GAME THEORY

A Very Brief and Non-Technical Introduction

GAME THEORY

A Very Brief and Non-Technical Introduction

Nejat Anbarci
Durham University, UK

Kemal Kıvanç Aköz
HSE University, Russia

Illustrations by Ergun Akleman

W&̂ World Scientific

NEW JERSEY · LONDON · SINGAPORE · BEIJING · SHANGHAI · TAIPEI · CHENNAI

Published by

World Scientific Publishing Europe Ltd.

57 Shelton Street, Covent Garden, London WC2H 9HE

Head office: 5 Toh Tuck Link, Singapore 596224

USA office: 27 Warren Street, Suite 401-402, Hackensack, NJ 07601

Library of Congress Control Number: 2025011024

British Library Cataloguing-in-Publication Data
A catalogue record for this book is available from the British Library.

GAME THEORY
A Very Brief and Non-Technical Introduction

ISBN 978-1-80061-764-3 (hardcover)
ISBN 978-1-80061-775-9 (paperback)
ISBN 978-1-80061-765-0 (ebook for institutions)
ISBN 978-1-80061-766-7 (ebook for individuals)

For any available supplementary material, please visit
https://www.worldscientific.com/worldscibooks/10.1142/Q0520#t=suppl

Desk Editors: Kannan Krishnan/Gabriel Rawlinson/Shi Ying Koe

Typeset by Stallion Press
Email: enquiries@stallionpress.com

Foreword

"Wait! I was going to eat that!" I thought, stunned, as he casually said, "Alright," and grabbed the last slice of pizza. I had arrived in the United States barely a week ago, fresh off the plane and still adjusting to the cultural differences. He was an American I had just met, hosting the party I was attending, and I couldn't help but stare in mild disbelief. In Turkey, such an exchange would have played out very differently. A polite refusal on my part, followed by an insistent offer on his, and maybe a playful back-and-forth until I finally accepted. That's "naz" – a subtle cultural ritual where generosity meets courtesy. But here, in the United States, I quickly learned the "equilibrium" was entirely different. No second offers, no insistence – just efficient decision-making.

It was 1992, and I had just arrived in Buffalo, N.Y., a fresh-faced Ph.D. student in economics. I was there thanks to Nejat Anbarci, one of the authors of this book, who helped me navigate my way from computer engineering to economics, Turkey to the United States. His encouragement, generosity, and belief in my potential made those leaps possible. Though we had never met in person, his guidance and support showed the kind of thoughtfulness and dedication that mark both a great mentor and a brilliant scholar.

Fast forward to today, I am a chaired professor of economics, an elected Fellow of the Game Theory Society, and an associate editor of several journals including the *International Journal of Game Theory*. I don't mention these to boast but to assure you, dear reader, that I know a rigorous and insightful book on game theory when I see one. This book by Nejat Anbarci and Kıvanç Aköz is not only rigorous but also accessible, engaging, and entertaining – a rare feat in a field often dominated by equations and abstractions.

Every interaction in life, from the mundane to the monumental, involves some degree of strategy. Whether we are negotiating a salary, deciding on the best route to take during rush hour, or even deciding who is going to eat the last slice of pizza, we constantly navigate a world of interdependent decisions. This is the realm of game theory, the study of strategic interactions – a field as fascinating as it is practical.

This book by Anbarci and Aköz opens the door to the intriguing world of game theory in a way that is both approachable and illuminating. It is not your typical academic tome filled with dense equations and intimidating jargon. Instead, it is a delightfully written, lighthearted exploration of complex ideas, designed to captivate a wide audience. Through stories, examples, and even playful illustrations, the authors bring game theory to life, showing how its concepts manifest in everyday life, business, politics, and even sports.

Math is the language of game theory, but, let's face it, not everyone finds math comforting. The book reassures readers right from the start: this is not a text that will scare anyone with dense formulas or equations. Take, for instance, the humorous anecdote of a woman mistaking Guido Menzio's mathematical notes for a terrorist code (see The "Prisoner's Dilemma" Game: The Terrorist Professor?). While math is indispensable for understanding game theory, Anbarci and Aköz strike a remarkable balance, presenting rigorous ideas with minimal reliance on mathematical expressions.

What makes this book truly exceptional is its reliance on stories. The authors believe – and rightly so – that the best way to appreciate theory is to see it in action. Through vivid stories, thoughtful examples, and a touch of humour, the authors bring game theory to life making complex ideas accessible to a wide audience without losing any of the depth. From Roberto Baggio's infamous missed penalty in the 1994 World Cup final, to the strategic maneuvers of the OPEC oil cartel, to the philosophical undertones of *The Matrix*, this book uses vivid, real-world examples to explain abstract concepts. The result is an engaging narrative that entertains as much as it educates. Delightful illustrations add an extra layer of fun. Readers even discover tidbits like the authors' prestigious Erdős numbers (3 and 4) and the illustrator's Erdős number of 2 – academic credentials cleverly woven into the book's charming visuals.

The authors take readers on a carefully structured journey, beginning with a wide range of classic and modern game theory models, such as the Prisoner's Dilemma, Battle of the Sexes, auctions, guessing games, and signalling and screening games. Each concept is introduced with clarity and precision, while the explanations remain intuitive and grounded in real-world scenarios. As the book progresses, it moves from simpler ideas like dominant strategies to more sophisticated concepts, such as equilibrium in games with imperfect information. This pedagogical flow mirrors the structure of a graduate-level game theory course, making the book invaluable even for advanced students.

Among the many admirable aspects of the book, its intellectual humility is worth noting. The authors resist presenting game theory as a universal solution for understanding human behaviour. Instead, they acknowledge its limitations, recognizing that real-life decisions are rarely made by perfectly rational, self-interested players, as emotions, fairness, and randomness often play significant roles in shaping outcomes. In this context, they also explore advanced topics such as the cognitive hierarchy model and behavioural economics.

For those new to game theory, the book offers a gentle and inviting introduction. For more advanced readers, it provides fresh insights and a deeper appreciation of the field's practical relevance. Whether you are a curious reader or a seasoned scholar, this book has something to offer. It's a rare gem, much like the man who once helped me start my own journey in this fascinating field.

Hülya Eraslan
Ralph O'Connor Professor of Economics
Rice University, Texas, USA

Preface

Welcome to the fascinating and curious world of game theory – also known as "the science of strategy". Over the last eighty years, game theory has quietly infiltrated into many disciplines, such as politics, economics, and even biology. That is no coincidence. Every aspect of social life, even romantic relationships, and pretty much anything involving more than one person contains some strategic element.

The choices we make every day are more interconnected than we often realize. Imagine a world where everything, from what cereal you choose in the morning to how countries negotiate peace, can be explained by clever moves and counter-moves. Game theory is all about that. Whether you're trying to outwit your rivals or keep your friends close and your frenemies even closer, it's a playground of strategies.

We believe that learning should be fun, not painful. Even the most complicated subjects can be communicated – to some degree – to a wide audience in an enjoyable way. Game theory should not be an exception even if it can get intense when you dive deep enough.

The goal of this book is to help you understand what game theory is without making you feel like you need an advanced degree in mathematics or a secret decoder ring. This little book won't overwhelm you with equations or complex jargon. Instead, it's filled with stories – simple yet sometimes quirky tales – that gently unwrap the hidden strategic dimension behind human behaviour. We are going to keep things simple – think of this as a friendly conversation over coffee where we sneak in a little math, but only the basic arithmetic operations.

We chose to convey the ideas through stories instead of abstract models since stories have a way of infusing lessons into our minds without the burden of technical explanations. They are memorable, fun, and often far more relatable than abstract concepts. After all, life is full of games. From bargaining for the last slice of pizza to outwitting your sibling in a family board game, we're constantly playing – whether we know it or not.

This book is written for anyone who wants to learn about the basics of game theory. Whether you are a student taking a course in economic theory, or just curious about why that one friend of yours always seems to win at Monopoly (spoiler alert: they've been using strategic thinking against you for years), we believe that you will find this book useful.

In each chapter, we introduce a key concept in game theory. We start with some of the best-known static games, where everyone acts at the same time, and move on to dynamic games, where there are sequential moves. However, before starting our journey, we have included two chapters immediately following the Introduction to showcase the wide-ranging applications of game theory in practical scenarios. The first explores a referee assignment mechanism that could be adopted by top football leagues, such as the English Premier League. This system incorporates teams' preferences for referees, creating a more transparent and balanced selection process. The second section introduces an AI-driven approach to address the rising prevalence of draws in chess. This mechanism evaluates each move by calculating its proximity to the "optimal move" as determined by powerful chess engines. The closer a player's move is to this optimal standard, the higher their quality score. In the event of a draw, the player with the higher cumulative quality score is declared the winner, encouraging precision and strategy throughout the match.

Now, we can't talk about game theory without mentioning its biggest celebrity: John Nash. You might remember him from the movie *A Beautiful Mind* (or, if you haven't seen it, it's a great watch – Russell Crowe stars, and there's math and drama). Nash was not just any mathematician; he was *that* brilliant, eccentric guy who made the rest of us look like we were still learning our multiplication tables. At 19, while most of us were busy figuring out how to live on instant noodles, Nash was already publishing papers. By 22, he had written his groundbreaking work that changed the field forever – and this was before he'd even finished his Ph.D! He was a little busy revolutionizing how we think about strategy and equilibrium.

Of course, Nash's story also includes a lot of struggles, as he battled paranoid schizophrenia for nearly thirty years before returning to his research. He went on to win the Nobel Prize in Economics in 1994.

This book is, in part, a tribute to Nash and his extraordinary contributions, with a little personal connection thrown in. Nejat Anbarci, one of the authors of this book, received a letter from Nash many years ago. It was a small but unforgettable gesture – one that still resonates today. You'll find that letter at the end of the book.

In short, we wrote this book with the same excitement Nash probably felt when he cracked the code on strategic thinking, and we hope you feel that energy and joy as you read it.

This book is designed to be a light, enjoyable, and almost math-free read that will give you a fresh perspective on the games we play in life, without ever requiring you to break out a calculator. By the end, you might just find yourself seeing everyday situations in a new strategic light – perhaps even with a smile.

So, grab a cup of coffee (or tea, if that's more your style), make yourself comfortable, get curious, and let's dive into the world of game theory, one story at a time. We promise it'll be more fun than you think!

Happy reading!

About the Authors

Nejat Anbarci was born in Istanbul in 1959. He obtained his undergraduate and master's degrees from Bogazici University (Istanbul, Turkey) in business administration (1982) and economics (1985), respectively. He was awarded a Ph.D degree in economics by the University of Iowa (USA) in 1988. He first served as an assistant professor at the State University of New York at Buffalo during 1988–1995; he then served as an associate professor and a full professor at the Florida International University during 1995–2008 and as a professor at Deakin University (Melbourne, Australia) during 2008–2018. Since 2018, he has been serving as a professor at Durham University in the UK. Dr. Anbarci also served as the department head of Economics and Finance at Durham University (2019–2021) and the department head of Economics at Deakin University (2010–2012). His research interests are microeconomics, game theory, bargaining theory, behavioural economics, experimental economics, and the political economy of natural disasters, among others. He has published in journals such as the *Quarterly Journal of Economics, Management Science*, the *International Economic Review*, and the *Journal of Economic Theory*. Dr. Anbarci has received major grants from funding agencies such as the Australian Research Council and the Social Science Research Council. His Erdős number is 3.

Kemal Kıvanç Aköz was born in Istanbul in 1983. After receiving his bachelor's degree (2005) and master's degree (2007) in economics from Bilkent University, he completed his Ph.D in economics at New York University in 2014. Until 2018, he worked as a postdoctoral research fellow at New York University Abu Dhabi in the United Arab Emirates. Since 2018, he has been working as an assistant professor at HSE University (Moscow) in Russia. His Erdős number is 4. He primarily conducts theoretical research in the fields of game theory, political economy, and matching theory.

Contents

Chapter 1

Introduction

1.1. The Emergence of Game Theory: 1944–1951

The fact that game theory emerged as a new field in the 1940s – during and in the aftermath of World War II – is no accident. Humanity was terrified by its capacity for self-destruction. At one point, the nuclear stockpile reached a level that could have blown the world up multiple times. Yet, while we were busy creating all these weapons of mass destruction, there wasn't a scientific method to help countries analyze and develop policies to avoid conflicts that involved such catastrophic possibilities. The development of advanced mathematical techniques and the initiative of some of the brightest minds in history helped the emergence of game theory as a tool for this purpose. Even in its earliest days, game theory made impressive strides, and that momentum has carried it forward ever since. In fact, over the past 30 years, more than 20 Nobel Prizes have gone to scientists contributing to this field.

The book that really launched the journey of game theory was *Theory of Games and Economic Behavior*, published in 1944 by John von Neumann and Oscar Morgenstern. John von Neumann was born in 1903 in Hungary but later became an American citizen. He was a mathematician, physicist, computer scientist, and engineer all rolled into one. He laid the groundwork for computer science and artificial intelligence, helped develop nuclear weapons, and even led the team that created the first computerized weather forecast. This guy was so brilliant that some Nobel Prize-winning physicists said he was even sharper than Einstein.[1]

Before von Neumann and Morgenstern's book came along, there were a few scientists who contributed to the field of game theory. Back in the 19th century, French mathematicians such as Antoine Augustin Cournot and Joseph Louis François Bertrand made the first contributions with their models for market analysis. Later, in the early 20th century, mathematicians such as Émile Borel, Ernst Zermelo, and Dénes Kőnig should also be counted.

Then came the big leap in the 1950s, courtesy of John Nash. As mentioned before, you might know him from the movie *A Beautiful Mind*, in which Russell Crowe made math look intense and emotional. Nash's second paper, published in 1951, gave us the Nash equilibrium, the most important solution concept in game theory. Nash's paper is now considered the most fundamental work in the field. These days, Nash equilibrium is so ingrained in scientific research that nobody even bothers to cite Nash anymore when they use it – it's just taken as a given.

The year 1950 gave us something else: the Prisoner's Dilemma. This game, born during the Cold War's nuclear arms race, didn't just answer unresolved questions; it changed how economists think about competition and cooperation. Its main conclusion that the self-interest of individuals might lead to the demise of the collective made some economists question some of the most common conclusions of economic theory at that time.

Over time, game theory has influenced everything from electrical and computer engineering to biology, psychology, and even ethics. Game theory was revolutionary, with its contributions reaching as far as evolutionary

---

[1] Bhattacharya, A. (October 2021). *The Spectator*, https://www.spectator.co.uk/article/the-forgotten-einstein-how-john-von-neumann-shaped-the-modern-world/.

psychology. Now, policy applications of game theory range from creating new markets to innovations in the field of kidney and liver transplantation, saving thousands of lives. In less than 80 years, game theory has transformed into one of the most important methods used across the scientific universe.

1.2. The Foundation of Game Theory: Strategic Interaction

Despite what the word "game" might suggest, game theory isn't merely about winning at sports or competitive games. No, it's about analyzing all kinds of strategic behaviour and interaction. In fact, a better name for it might be the "Science of Strategy." Whether you're planning a major business deal or figuring out who's going to do the dishes, chances are you're engaging in some form of game theory. Nearly every interaction we have in modern life involves strategy. Unlike poor Robinson Crusoe, who spent most of his time on a deserted island worrying only about coconuts and survival, today's individuals face much more complex choices: decisions about their social lives, careers, parenting, and much more. All these decisions are influenced by the potential choices of others who, more often than not, have different goals.

In every strategic scenario, there are players, and each player has strategies. Players try to choose the strategy that will give them the best possible outcome given what the other players are doing. Sometimes, the other players are opponents, sometimes allies, and sometimes both. For example, a "game" might involve figuring out when and where two long-distance lovers can meet again, or it could be a simple decision about which restaurant to pick for their long-awaited reunion.

A game can be straightforward, such as chess or tennis, where the rules are clear, and everyone knows them. However, it can also be ambiguous, like deciding who's responsible for changing diapers or tackling household chores. Bargaining with a jeweller at a bazaar requires a strategy to get the best deal from someone whom you know, possibly because you negotiated with them before. Even changing lanes on your drive home from work involves strategy – you're making decisions based on how you think other drivers (whom you don't know and will probably never meet) are going to behave.

Nonetheless, games aren't merely limited to individuals. Two companies deciding how to price their products are playing a game against each other, just as two nations do when figuring out how much they should invest in armaments or how to tackle pollution.

From this perspective, strategic thinking is something everyone should learn – and practice. It's not only for sports such as football, basketball, or chess. In fact, it's a key to success in all walks of life. Businesspeople need to master strategies to stay competitive, and politicians need smart strategies to win votes and deliver on their promises.

Successfully predicting the outcome of any game depends on two things: how rational the players are and how well they understand the rules. The clearer the rules and the more logical the players, the easier it is to predict who's going to come out on top. However, even when everything seems predictable, there's always room for a surprise. Players might have several best strategies against others' expected play, and that might lead to multiple solutions (equilibria) of the game. Finally, random factors might induce further uncertainty.

1.3. A Real-Life Example of Strategy: Baggio's Penalty

Let's dive back into the heart of any game: strategy. In many situations, people make decisions based on a carefully crafted plan of action, designed to achieve their goals. We know the world is filled with others who have their own goals, which often don't align with ours, so we're always trying to figure out the best moves to make in any given situation. It's like a mental chess game – predicting which strategies will work and which won't. Of course, even the best plans can fail due to some unforeseen factors.

PENALTY KICKS

THE FIRST GAME THEORIST GOALKEEPER

DISCOVERED THAT RANDOMLY CHOOSING A DIRECTION AND DIVING WAS THE BEST STRATEGY.

THE FIRST GAME THEORIST STRIKER

DISCOVERED THAT THE BEST STRATEGY AGAINST GOALKEEPERS WHO DIVE RANDOMLY IS TO LEAVE THE BALL IN THE MIDDLE.

CZECH FOOTBALLER ANTONÍN PANENKA INVENTED THE PENALTY KICK TECHNIQUE NAMED AFTER HIM IN 1976. IN THIS TECHNIQUE, THE PLAYER LIGHTLY TOUCHES THE BALL UNDERNEATH TO LIFT IT AND SLOWLY ROLLS IT TOWARDS THE CENTER OF THE GOAL. A GOALKEEPER DIVING TO THE RIGHT OR LEFT CANNOT SAVE THE BALL. ALTHOUGH IT WAS EFFECTIVE WHEN FIRST INVENTED, IT HAS BEEN OBSERVED THAT PENALTIES TAKEN WITH THE PANENKA KICK NO LONGER HAVE A VERY HIGH PROBABILITY OF SCORING

To illustrate how strategies can play out in real life, let's look at an iconic moment in sports history: Roberto Baggio's infamous missed penalty in the 1994 World Cup final. In his autobiography, Baggio recounts that moment:

> I don't want to brag, but I'd only missed two penalties in my entire career before that. And both misses were because the goalkeeper saved them, not because I kicked the ball out. I knew that Brazil's goalkeeper, Taffarel, never stayed in the middle of the goal during penalties; he always picked a corner and dove. So, I figured I would aim dead centre – right down the middle, both horizontally and vertically – where his feet wouldn't reach. It was the perfect plan, as

Taffarel dove to his left, and he'd never have saved the penalty I planned. But somehow – the ball shot three meters into the air and sailed over the crossbar. I failed. Period. It was the worst moment of my career. If I could erase one moment from my career, it would be this one.

This short but telling passage offers several valuable lessons about strategy and its outcomes. First, we see that Baggio based his move on Taffarel's past strategy. He knew Taffarel liked to pick a side and dive, rather than standing in the middle and reacting. If Taffarel had been the kind of goalkeeper who stayed central and moved only after the ball's direction became clear, Baggio would likely never have aimed his penalty down the middle.

Second, Taffarel's strategy – picking a corner and diving – was no accident. It takes about 0.2 seconds for a goalkeeper to see the ball, figure out where it's going, and start moving. However, that's almost the same amount of time it takes for the ball to reach the goal; so, most goalkeepers have adopted the strategy of anticipating where the ball might go and diving towards that direction before the shot even comes. This tactic has been the subject of serious research. And before this penalty, Taffarel likely made some educated guesses – perhaps Baggio had a tendency to aim left, or maybe he picked up clues from Baggio's body language just before the kick.

Third, top-level footballers know that even when a goalkeeper dives towards a corner, there's a small chance they'll save a shot aimed at the centre, especially ground-level shots. Baggio clearly thought through this risk, and yet he decided the middle was the safest bet. He even factored in the *small chance* that Taffarel might stretch out a foot and block the shot.

And finally, let's not forget about luck. Maybe it was nerves, maybe Baggio's foot caught the ball slightly wrong, or maybe the field was a bit soft and slippery in that spot – whatever the reason, the ball didn't go where Baggio intended. Instead, it soared into the sky, leaving Italy's World Cup dreams shattered. So, no matter how well planned the strategy, the element of chance can still throw everything off.

One last important point to note is that, in games, the players are rarely on equal footing. One side usually has more information, better skills, or some other kind of advantage. In Baggio's case, Taffarel had the advantage of knowing Baggio's tendencies, while Baggio felt the pressure of knowing that the entire World Cup hinged on his kick. We'll delve into these kinds of unequal situations in more detail in the final chapters.

1.4. Testing the Validity of Game Theory: Behavioural Economics

Before we dive any deeper, let's clear something up: this book is all about game theory, but it's not here to worship it. Like everything beautiful, game theory also comes with its flaws. In its classic, widely used form, it assumes that we're all like Mr. Spock from *Star Trek* – coldly logical, relying only on the cortex part of our brains. But we humans have some extra baggage. Along with our cortex, we've got the mammalian brain (which prioritizes emotions) and the reptilian brain (which handles our more primitive instincts). Our emotions, gut reactions, and general inconsistencies play a huge role in our decision-making.

This is why we need to test the "cortex-only" assumptions of game theory. Behavioural economics has been quietly developing over the past 40 years, helping to keep game theory in check. Game theory assumes that everyone is laser-focused on their own self-interest and doesn't care about anyone else's gains or feelings. However, most of us are always comparing what we are getting to what others are getting. Behavioural economics steps in to show us just how far from perfect that cold, rational view can be.

Take, for example, the ultimatum game (which we'll dig into in Chapter 10 "The Ultimatum Game: Mr. Charles' Will"). It's simple: one person makes an offer to another about how to split a sum of money. The second person can say yes and accept the offer or say no and both walk away with nothing. Now, in the world of game theory, the proposer would offer the smallest possible amount (say, 5–10 pennies), and the other person would accept it, because a little bit is better than nothing.

Nevertheless, thousands of experiments tell a different story. Behavioural economics shows us that, in reality, the second person isn't just a calculating robot. If the proposer doesn't offer at least around 40% of the total, the offer is often rejected out of principle, and the proposer knows this. So, instead of trying to lowball the offer, they aim for something fairer. This is one of many ways behavioural economics keeps game theory grounded.

Another example is the famous Prisoner's Dilemma, which we'll talk about in the following chapter. In theory, this game often ends in a disappointing outcome: both players lose out due to mistrust. But in real-world settings, under the right conditions, players often find ways to cooperate and achieve better results. It's one more reason why we can't ignore the human element in strategic thinking.

As we continue, we'll see more instances where behavioural economics – the "Dionysian" side of human decision-making helps to temper the "Apollonian" logic of game theory. It turns out, we're not just self-interested robots; real-life decisions involve emotions, fairness, and sometimes even random, inexplicable choices.

So, to all our readers setting sail into the exciting waters of game theory, here's a word of advice: "Don't challenge anyone without reading this book first!" And enjoy the journey in the land of game theory, where you can also see the colourful flowers of behavioural economics.

Chapter 2

Referee Appointments in Fantasia: An Algorithm Based on Fair Play and Harmony

Matching theory examines how to pair agents (such as individuals, resources, or institutions) in a way that optimizes a desired outcome, such as efficiency, stability, or fairness. It addresses questions like assigning students to schools, workers to jobs, or donors to recipients of organ donation. Assignment problems are a subset of matching theory focused on finding the best one-to-one matches between two sets, like tasks and workers, where each pair has an associated cost or value. Often, the aim is to minimize costs or maximize benefits while ensuring that each entity is matched appropriately.

Matching theory and assignment problems are closely related to game theory because they involve agents with preferences or objectives that may conflict. Game theory provides a framework for understanding how agents make decisions and interact strategically in matching scenarios. For instance, in matching markets for school admissions or job placements, stability appears as a key concept. Akin to the equilibrium concepts in game theory, stability describes matchings where no couple of agents prefers to deviate. One of the most well-known mechanisms, the Gale–Shapley algorithm, achieves stable outcomes where no pair would prefer to deviate. Concepts like strategy-proofness, where agents have no incentive to misrepresent their preferences, are crucial in designing matching mechanisms.

Following is a story about a particular assignment problem, the assignment of referees to football matches. The story is based on a recent research project that one of the authors of this book (Nejat Anbarci) and his collaborators have contributed to.[1] The project offers a new referee-matching mechanism that could potentially be useful for the English Premier League's referee appointment methods.

******

In the enchanting nation of Fantasia, football was more than just a sport. It was a tapestry of passion, culture, and identity. The people of Fantasia lived and breathed the beautiful game, filling their cities with chants, flags, and boundless energy on matchdays. But beneath this joy, a shadow loomed controversy over referee appointments.

The stakes in Fantasia's Supreme Football League (SFL) were immense. Championships and relegations often hung by a thread, and fans scrutinized every whistle, every card, every decision. Allegations of referee bias had become routine, with teams and fans blaming perceived favouritism for their losses. Media outlets fanned the flames, turning referee decisions into national debates. The once-glorious game was at risk of losing its shine.

Realizing the urgency of the matter, the Supreme Football Federation of Fantasia (SFFF) called an emergency council. The greatest minds in Fantasia's footballing community were summoned. Among those were a trio

---

[1] That project, entitled "Arbiter assignment", is to appear in the journal entitled *Social Choice and Welfare* in 2025.

of researchers and innovators: the professor of economics Zephyros Star-weaver, the engineer Lyric Solaria, and the AI pioneer Elara Moonforge. They had a solution that could address the problem of favouritism and its perception among the fans once and for all. Intrigued by the proposal, the council members invited them to give a speech to describe their solution.

THIS WOULDN'T EVEN BE CALLED A FOUL. REFEREE, YOU WON'T BE ALLOWED BACK IN THIS STADIUM AGAIN!

AAARGH!

ERGUN AKLEMAN

IN FANTASIA'S SUPREME FOOTBALL LEAGUE, SOME FANS BELIEVE THAT EVEN IF ONE OF THEIR PLAYERS COMMITS A SERIOUS CRIME PUNISHABLE BY LAW, THE REFEREE SHOULD STILL REFRAIN FROM PENALIZING THEIR PLAYER.

Zephyros stepped forward. "Honored council members," he began, "The chaos surrounding referee appointments is a problem not of fairness but of perception. And perception," he paused, "can be reshaped through science." Lyric smiled and took over. "We're here to introduce a solution that has worked in fields as critical as healthcare and education. Today, we adapt it to the game we all cherish." Elara added, "This is not just about solving disputes. It's about restoring faith in our game."

The trio painted a vivid picture of the crisis. Teams in Fantasia had strong opinions about referees, often based on their past decisions, competence, or perceived biases. "Referees are human," Lyric said. "And humans are fallible. They face social pressure, crowd influence, and subconscious biases." Ignoring team preferences only exacerbated the problem. Fans and players alike felt unheard, leading to heated debates and declining trust in the system. The randomness of referee assignments wasn't working. A new approach was desperately needed – one that respected team preferences while maintaining fairness and neutrality.

The researchers unveiled their solution: the *Depth Optimal Priority (DOP)* algorithm. This was an adaptation of systems that had revolutionized organ transplants, student placements, and even peace negotiations.

Zephyros explained the process:

1. **Weekly Setup:** Each week, the *Council of Whistling Stars* – Fantasia's supreme refereeing body – would list the referees available for matches.
2. **Team Preferences:** Teams would rank referees in order of preference using a secure, magical program. These rankings could remain private if the teams wished.
3. **Match Importance:** The SFFF would rank matches based on importance, considering public interest, team standings, and stakes involved. A clash between title contenders or a relegation battle, for instance, would rank higher than mid-table encounters.
4. **Referee Assignment:** Using the *Unanimity Compromise (UC) procedure*, the DOP algorithm would assign referees to matches, starting with the most critical games. Once assigned, referees were removed from the pool for that week.

Elara took over. "This method," she explained, "is rooted in the principle of harmony. It balances the preferences of both teams, ensuring fairness and efficiency."

To illustrate, she conjured an example: The home team ranked referees as Aurelian, Bryndor, Caelus, Dainar, and Elidor, while the visiting team ranked them as Caelus, Elidor, Dainar, Bryndor, and Aurelian. The UC procedure evaluated each referee by their worst ranking between the two teams. For instance:

- **Aurelian** was ranked first by the home team but fifth by the visitors, so his worst ranking was fifth.
- **Caelus**, ranked third by the home team and first by the visitors, had a worst ranking of third.
- The algorithm selected *Caelus* because his worst ranking (third) was better than the others.

"This ensures fairness, because no referee could make both teams happier simultaneously," she added.

The researchers emphasized the far-reaching benefits of the DOP algorithm:

- **Fairness:** By considering team preferences, the algorithm minimized feelings of bias.
- **Transparency:** The process was clear, leaving little room for conspiracy theories or backroom dealings.
- **Efficiency:** Referees were assigned in a way that maximized satisfaction without compromising the league's integrity.

"The DOP algorithm," declared Professor Starweaver, "isn't just a tool. It's a promise to every player, fan, and referee in Fantasia: that football will be fair, beautiful, and free from unnecessary controversy."

The presentation was convincing. The council voted unanimously to adopt the system for the next season. When the algorithm debuted in the Supreme Football League, it was an instant success. Referee controversies dwindled. Players, coaches, and fans began to trust the system once more, focusing their energy on the game rather than its officiating. This success of the algorithm inspired leagues across the world to adopt similar systems.

Chapter 3

The Grand Chess Saga of Fantasia: The Rise of the Wise Machine

The following story is based on the recent academic work of one of the authors of this book (Nejat Anbarci) with one of his co-authors.[1] It intends to provide a very practical solution to the overwhelming trend of draws in chess.

******

3.1. A Game of Starlight and Strategy

Chess, at its core, is a battle of minds. Despite its apparent complexity, it falls into the category of *dynamic games* which are covered in the second half of this book. And though chess has been played for centuries, the famous *Zermelo's theorem (1913)* tells us something curious – with perfect play, one of three outcomes is guaranteed:

1. Player 1 (White) can force a win.
2. Player 2 (Black) can force a win.
3. Both players can force a draw (if both play perfectly).

---

[1] That project entitled "AI-powered mechanisms as judges: Breaking ties in chess" appeared in the journal entitled *PLOS One* in November 2024.

The true "solution" to chess is still unknown, and therein lies its magic. The uncertainty keeps players captivated, each match is a new adventure. However, draw is not an ending favoured by everyone. Just ask the people of Fantasia.

In Fantasia, chess was more than a game – it was a sacred dance of intellect. From the enchanted villages of the Emerald Vale to the gleaming towers of the Crystal Citadel, chess united people from every corner of the realm. The Tournament of the Grandmasters was the crown jewel of these gatherings, an annual spectacle that drew spectators in, just like moths to a magical flame.

But over time, something went wrong. The excitement waned. Draws. Draws everywhere. The 2018 tournament was the most infamous of them all – 12 consecutive draws. Fans grumbled. Players groaned. Even squirrels, who had gathered to watch, threw acorns in protest. The dreaded tiebreakers, once seen as a necessary evil, were now the object of scorn. Fast-paced, frantic blitz matches left little room for strategy or brilliance. It felt more like a race than a battle of minds.

The realm demanded change. The Council of the Eternal Mind, guardians of Fantasia's intellectual heritage, knew they had to act. They turned to two of the most brilliant minds in the land:

- **Professor Eryndor Starflame**, a sage with an unmatched mastery of strategy and fairness, known for his calm wisdom and a beard so long it had its own chapter in the archives.
- **Maestra Velora Aetherwind**, an inventor of boundless creativity who had built enchanted machines to solve Fantasia's most puzzling dilemmas (including the "Mystery of the Disappearing Tea Biscuits" incident of 1473).

On a crisp autumn morning, in the grand chambers of the Crystal Observatory, Starflame and Aetherwind revealed their grand idea. Beneath a dome of enchanted crystal that shimmered like a dragonfly's wing, the two scholars faced the Council of the Eternal Mind, a semi-circle of watchful elders and strategists.

"Honoured members of the council," began Starflame, his voice as steady as a metronome, "chess is a game of precision, creativity, and foresight. But in recent years, our cherished game has been tarnished. Rapid tiebreakers—though necessary at the time—have stripped chess of its soul. They reward speed over strategy, chaos over calculation."

At this, several councillors nodded grimly. One elder muttered, "My granddaughter can move faster than these so-called champions."

Maestra Aetherwind stepped forward, her emerald robes shimmering with enchantments. She held up a glowing orb, pulsing with a soft, rhythmic light. "Behold: The Wise Machine," she declared, and the crowd gasped. The orb floated in the air, its glow syncing perfectly with the gentle pulse of the chamber's enchanted lanterns.

"This machine," she continued, "combines the wisdom of ancient texts with the precision of enchanted algorithms. It evaluates every move in a chess game, comparing it to the best possible play. It assigns a quality score to each move, rewarding creativity, foresight, and precision."

The council leaned forward; eyes wide with curiosity. "How does it work?" asked Grandmaster Felnor the Flawless, a chess champion so skilled that rooks were said to move out of his way out of respect.

Aetherwind grinned. "Simple, yet profound," she said. "For every move, the Wise Machine calculates how close it is to the 'optimal move.' The closer it is, the higher the quality score. At the end of a match, if a draw occurs, the player with the highest score wins. No more tiebreakers. No more racing the clock. Every move matters."

The murmurs in the council grew louder. "This could change everything," one whispered. Another added, "No more 'play-for-the-draw' strategies. Now, players will have to strive for excellence in every move."

"Ah," said a wizened elder, raising his hand. "But what of manipulation? Players have always found ways to twist the rules in their favour. If they once played for tiebreakers, they would find a way to exploit this system too."

Starflame's eyes twinkled. "Not this time, elder." He stood with his hands behind his back, like a teacher waiting for students to see the obvious. "The Wise Machine rewards precision, not results. No player can coast to a draw and hope to win. If you play lazily, your quality score will plummet. Excellence will be the only path to victory."

"No shortcuts?" asked the elder.

"None," said Aetherwind, arms crossed with confidence. "Every. Move. Matters."

The room fell silent. The council stared at the two scholars, then at the glowing orb. Slowly, but surely, smiles began to spread.

With unanimous approval, The Wise Machine was installed at the Tournament of the Grand Kings. The announcement sent ripples of excitement through Fantasia. Fans, players, and squirrels alike eagerly awaited the results. Would it work? Could it truly restore the heart of chess?

With the machine judging every move, players had to bring their A-game from the first move to the last. Gone were the sluggish, low-risk moves aimed at forcing draws. Instead, matches were now a display of daring sacrifices, bold advances, and clever gambits. Even draws became thrilling.

When a match ended in a draw, The Wise Machine's soft glow brightened as it declared the true winner. The announcement was clear, fair, and, most importantly, undeniable.

The Wise Machine's influence didn't stop with chess. Its principles found use in other competitions:

- **Archery contests:** The machine scored shots not just on accuracy but also on the strategy behind each shot.
- **Duels of wit:** In these verbal battles, poets and philosophers sparred with words, and The Wise Machine judged which arguments were clever, sharp, and sound.

- **Alchemy trials:** Even potions were judged for their balance, originality, and sheer brilliance. No more "accidental" explosions that happened to be judged "creative."

As the twin moons rose above the Crystal Citadel, their light reflected off banners bearing the sigil of the Tournament of the Grandmasters. Chess, once burdened by controversy, had been reborn as a celebration of skill, strategy, and artistry. The game was now fair. Every move had meaning. Every player had to earn their glory.

Professor Starflame, sitting on a bench near the tournament grounds, gazed at the moonlit chessboard. "It was never about who won," he said to a young apprentice. "It was about ensuring that brilliance was recognized."

Maestra Aetherwind, adjusting a few enchantments on a new contraption (possibly a self-sorting laundry basket), glanced over and grinned. "And this," she said, tapping her glowing machine, "is only the beginning."

As the people of Fantasia gathered for the next great match, the night air was filled with cheers, gasps, and laughter. Under the watchful glow of The Wise Machine, chess was no longer a game of dull draws and desperate tiebreakers. It was a stage for brilliance, courage, and artful play.

And as the stars winked down from the heavens, it seemed, just for a moment, that even they approved.

Chapter 4

The Most Iconic Game of All: The Prisoner's Dilemma

In the world of game theory, some strategies just outshine the rest. These are called "dominant" strategies – they guarantee a better outcome, no matter what your opponent throws at you. In other words, dominant strategies lead to the highest payoff or benefit, regardless of what the other player does. On the flip side, we have "dominated" strategies, which are inferior strategies. These are the strategies you don't want to use because no matter what your opponent does, there's always a better option you could have picked. Think of it like trying to kick the ball out of bounds during a penalty kick – it doesn't matter what the goalkeeper is doing, it's always worse than just aiming for the goal. Dominated strategies are pointless and bound to fail.

Now, not every game has dominant or dominated strategies. Sometimes, the waters are a little murkier. Also, dominant strategies don't have to be moral choices, and dominated strategies don't necessarily have to be evil. In fact, sometimes the roles are reversed. One classic example of this is the Prisoner's Dilemma, which we get into in the following. It shows that sometimes dominant strategy can lead to a result that leaves both players scratching their heads, wondering, "How did we end up here?"

4.1. The "Prisoner's Dilemma" Game: The Terrorist Professor?

It was a calm Thursday evening on May 5, 2016, when a 40-year-old man with curly dark hair, tanned skin, an exotic accent, and glasses boarded a flight from Philadelphia, USA, to Ontario, Canada. He had no clue that his upcoming journey would turn into something out of a comedy of errors. Meet Guido Menzio, a sharp, young economics professor from the University of Pennsylvania. Guido was heading to give a seminar at the University of Western Ontario, just another day in the life of an academic. Before take-off, he was already preoccupied with his seminar notes, fully focused on the equations in front of him.

But, unfortunately for Guido, this was a time when Donald Trump had just been elected president and xenophobia was starting to brew across the country. Seated next to Guido was a woman in her 30s, and something about

Guido – his focus on cryptic symbols – didn't sit right with her. In her mind, Guido's notes might as well have been terrorist codes. She decided to act on her worries and started an investigation of her own.

She tried to strike up a conversation with Guido, asking where he was going and what he was working on. But Guido, buried in his work, responded with a few vague, distracted answers. This only fuelled her suspicions. Convinced that she was sitting next to a terrorist mastermind, the woman informed the flight crew that she wanted to leave the plane and then, once safely back on the ground, reported the "Middle Eastern terrorist" to security.

Guido's flight was delayed by two hours, and he found himself being escorted off the plane by security officers for a little chat. We don't know exactly what was said during Guido's interrogation, but it was cleared up eventually, and the flight continued without incident.

So far, our story has been inspired by real-life events.[1] Now, to connect this story to the topic of this chapter, let's imagine a fictional economics professor named Alberto. Like Guido, Alberto was also taken off a plane and questioned by the FBI for the same reason. This is where things take an interesting turn, leading us to the Prisoner's Dilemma.

FBI Agent: "What are these codes, huh? What were you planning to blow up?"

Alberto: "These aren't codes! These are math formulas I'm using to prove the existence of Nash equilibrium!"

FBI Agent: "Is this Nash your cell leader?"

Alberto: "No, Nash is a respected mathematician!"

---

[1] https://www.washingtonpost.com/news/rampage/wp/2016/05/07/ivy-league-economist-interrogated-for-doing-math-on-american-airlines-flight/ .

Fast-forward to an hour later, and our overzealous FBI agents come back with smug expressions. "We've caught your pal Nash, and he's already confessed. So, spill the beans!" they say.

Of course, this Nash isn't the John Nash, one of the founders of game theory, but someone the FBI found who happens to be in a bit of trouble. Let's assume this person, "Nash," has committed minor crimes like theft, and the FBI has enough evidence to put him away for three years. Meanwhile, poor Alberto also has a minor offence – let's say he hit a parked car last month and fled the scene. The FBI's got the footage, and if they pursue it, he's in for a short prison sentence too.

Now, imagine both Alberto and Nash are being interrogated separately. The FBI gives them a choice: if both stay silent, they'll each serve three years. But if one confesses and the other denies, the confessor will be pardoned, and the silent one will get slapped with a 10-year sentence. If they both confess, they'll each get six years for their cooperation with the FBI.

Here's how their options look:

		Nash	
		Confess	Deny
Alberto	Confess	6 years, 6 years	0 years, 10 years
	Deny	10 years, 0 years	3 years, 3 years

The numbers in each cell show the prison terms for Alberto (row player) and Nash (column player). If Alberto confesses and Nash denies, Alberto goes free, and Nash gets 10 years (bottom left). If both confess, they get six years each (top left).

Now, let's imagine Alberto's thought process. Although he's pretty sure the Nash the FBI caught isn't the John Nash, he realizes that Nash is in a similar bind. Alberto knows they both have two options: confess or deny. If Nash confesses and Alberto denies, Alberto is looking at 10 long years behind bars. But if Alberto confesses too, they'll both be in for six years, which isn't great, but it's better than 10. Even if Nash stays silent, confessing could get Alberto off the hook entirely. So, after doing some quick mental math, Alberto decides confessing is the best strategy, the dominant strategy, no matter what Nash does.

Nash, meanwhile, is sitting in his own interrogation room, probably running through the same thoughts. He figures confessing is the safest bet too, and just like that the inevitable outcome is that both confess, leading to the so-called dominant equilibrium: six years each, instead of the more favourable three years had they both kept quiet.

In this classic Prisoner's Dilemma, both players realize they're stuck, and despite knowing that staying silent would give them a better collective outcome, they both confess to avoid the worst-case scenario. Therefore, both Alberto and Nash end up serving six years, probably cursing their bad luck along the way.

Side Note: In some popular game theory books, you'll come across other amusing fictional tales similar to the story we just described. One of the most famous stories goes something like this:

During the Stalin era in the Soviet Union, a conductor was travelling by train, on his way to conduct a concert. Naturally, as a good conductor does, he spent the journey meticulously reviewing the musical score for the piece he was set to perform that evening. But things took a surprising turn when two over-vigilant KGB agents happened to note his sheet music. To their suspicious minds, these weren't just harmless musical notes – they were obviously some kind of secret code! Convinced they had stumbled upon a spy; they swiftly arrested the conductor.

Despite the conductor's earnest protests that the sheet music was simply Tchaikovsky's violin concerto, it was no use. The KGB wasn't buying it. On the second day of his interrogation, one of the agents entered the room with a self-satisfied smirk and delivered the punchline: "You might as well confess now. We've already caught your accomplice, Tchaikovsky, and he's spilling everything."

4.2. Another Example of the "Prisoner's Dilemma" Game

Let's imagine a region where drought is in full swing, and everyone is being urged to conserve water. Now, if no one else is conserving water – and you don't exactly have a burning sense of moral duty to help out – then why not keep that water running? After all, if everyone else is slacking off, there's no immediate reason for you to suffer by taking shorter showers. After all, the drought will continue even if you conserve water. Similarly, if everyone else *is* dutifully conserving water, and you're still not particularly feeling the "save the planet" vibe, you might think, "Hey, now I've got even more water to myself! Jackpot!" Plus, let's be honest, especially if you're not the one paying the water bill, but it is included in the rent, the temptation is even stronger.

For a selfish person, this logic will always apply. Whether people are conserving water or not, *you* not conserving water will seem like the smartest move, providing the most personal benefit. This makes "not conserving water" a dominant strategy – it's the choice that gets you the most in the short term, regardless of what others do. But here's the kicker: if everyone plays the selfish card, eventually, we'll all be dealing with a water crisis of epic proportions. No one will have any water, and everyone will suffer. This is a situation where the dominant equilibrium is the collectively inferior outcome.

This type of situation is a perfect example of the Tragedy of the Commons: when individuals, acting in their own self-interest, end up depleting or

degrading shared resources, leaving everyone worse off. The policy response is often to restrict such selfish behaviour like the fishing restrictions designed to protect fish populations.

If you've already connected the dots, you'll see that this water conservation scenario is essentially the Prisoner's Dilemma but played out by society as a whole instead of just two people.

Now, just a quick side note. The examples we've been discussing might make it seem like game theory is encouraging everyone to go for short-term wins, even if it means shooting yourself (and everyone else) in the foot in the long run. But that's not the case. One of game theory's main goals is to analyze why people end up using these selfish strategies and to figure out how to break out of these damaging cycles. Alternatively, if there are multiple Nash equilibria (some good, some bad), game theory helps us understand how the policymakers can push things towards one of the better outcomes rather than getting stuck in a bad one.

4.3. A Real-Life Example: Why Is the OPEC Cartel Always Troublesome?

Since the early 1970s, the Organization of Petroleum Exporting Countries (OPEC) has been formed to raise the price of crude oil, which was shockingly low at that time at just three dollars per barrel. For a while, their efforts didn't seem to make much of a dent. But then along came the Arab–Israeli War of 1973, and everything changed. Most of OPEC's members were Arab countries that felt the West had turned against them during the war; so in response, they made a collective decision to hike up crude oil prices. Fast forward to the 1980s, and the price had skyrocketed to over $30 per barrel! The world began holding its breath every time OPEC met in Vienna to set new prices and quotas, as these decisions seemed to have the power to send economies into a tailspin.

But, like all cartels, OPEC started to lose its tight grip on oil prices in the 1980s. By early 1986, the price of oil had tumbled back down to a mere $10 per barrel. Relatively recently, in 2008, the oil prices dropped from $160 to around $50 a few years later and then climbed back up to $120 in April 2022 after the start of the Russia–Ukraine war. Sure, things like oil extraction costs and shifts in global demand played a role in these ups and downs like a roller coaster ride. However, in some cases, there are wild fluctuations even when there are no major changes in the global economic conditions. So, what's really going on here?

Like any cartel, OPEC faces a classic problem: the temptation to ditch long-term cooperation for short-term gains. Each member country knows that if they cheat a little on their quotas – pumping more oil than agreed – they can make some quick cash. The trouble is, if *everyone* starts doing this, the whole plan falls apart, and prices drop like a stone. Interestingly, the main strategic dilemma that OPEC countries face is entirely consistent with the one in the Prisoner's Dilemma.

Let's break it down with an example.

For simplicity, let's pretend OPEC is made up of only two members. These two countries control the world's oil, and the global annual demand for oil plays out as follows:

- $40 per barrel for 2 million barrels,
- $25 per barrel for 3 million barrels,
- $15 per barrel for 4 million barrels.

(We'll also just ignore the production costs for now. No need to complicate things further!)

Each country in our mini-OPEC has two production options: they can either pump out 1 million barrels per day (playing by the rules) or go rogue and pump 2 million barrels per day. If both countries behave and stick to the agreed quota of 1 million barrels each, the price will stay at $40 per barrel, and both countries will make a tidy $40 million.

But, if both countries decide to throw caution to the wind and produce 2 million barrels, the market will be flooded with oil. This causes the price to plummet to $15 per barrel, and their profits reduce to $30 million each. Now, that sounds like a disaster; so, at first glance, it seems like the logical choice would be for both countries to stick to their quotas.

There's another, sneakier option. What if one country sticks to the quota of 1 million barrels, but the other decides to secretly increase its production to

2 million barrels? In this case, daily production jumps to 3 million barrels, and the price falls to $25 per barrel. The poor country that stuck to the rules sees its profit fall to $25 million. Meanwhile, the country that decided to cheat and ramp up production enjoys a sweet profit of $50 million! Naturally, this makes it awfully tempting for both countries to break down the cooperation.

Let's break down the strategies of our two OPEC players. To keep things interesting, let's call the first country Iran and the second country Venezuela. Now, let's consider what happens when Iran plays by the rules and sticks to the 1 million barrels quota. If Venezuela also behaves and produces 1 million barrels, both countries will walk away with a nice profit of $40 million each. But if Venezuela decides to go rogue and bump up production to 2 million barrels, Venezuela's profit shoots up to $50 million while poor Iran is left with just $25 million. Clearly, the best move for Venezuela in this scenario is to break the quota.

Here's what that looks like:

		Venezuela	
		1 million barrels	2 million barrels
Iran	1 million barrels	$40 million, $40 million	$25 million, $50 million
	2 million barrels	$50 million, $25 million	$30 million, $30 million

Now, what if Iran decides to break the quota first and pumps out 2 million barrels? Well, if Venezuela sticks to the quota and produces 1 million barrels, the price will drop to $25 per barrel, leaving Venezuela with just $25 million. But if Venezuela also pumps out 2 million barrels, the price per barrel drops to $15, and both countries will make $30 million. So, breaking the quota is also Venezuela's best move when Iran is producing 2 million barrels.

In other words, no matter what Iran does, Venezuela makes more money by producing 2 million barrels. Producing only 1 million barrels is the dominated strategy here.

As this game is symmetric, the same logic applies to Iran. No matter what Venezuela does, Iran makes more money by producing 2 million barrels. For both countries, sticking to the 1-million-barrel quota is a dominated strategy. The only way forward for each is to pump out 2 million barrels, even though that leads to lower prices and profits for everyone.

******

For more mathematically inclined readers:

		Player 2	
		Cooperate	Defect
Player 1	Cooperate	(a,a)	(b,c)
	Defect	(c,b)	(d,d)
c>a>d>b			

The Prisoner's Dilemma often refers to any game where both players have a dominant strategy, but the outcome from following those strategies leaves them worse off than if they had chosen the dominated strategies. In other words, both players end up with lower payoffs by defecting than they would if they'd just cooperated. So, while they're technically playing it smart by choosing their dominant strategies, they're also shooting themselves in the foot. In these games, the only equilibrium outcome isn't – what is called – Pareto efficient. An outcome is called Pareto efficient if there is no other outcome that is not worse for all players, and it is strictly better for at least one player.

In the table above, if both players decide to cooperate, they each get the payoff of "a." But here's where the selfish temptation kicks in: the payoff "c" is better than "a," and "d" is better than "b," so the defect pays off better to both players. This makes defect the dominant strategy for both, even though it results in both players walking away with the lower payoff "d." If only they'd coordinated and chosen to cooperate, they could've each walked away with the higher payoff of "a" instead of settling for "d." Here, the "cooperate, cooperate" outcome is Pareto efficient; it dominates in this Pareto sense the "defect, defect" outcome.

In our earlier OPEC example, "a" was the $40 million both countries could earn if they cooperated. "b" was the $25 million one country gets while the other cheats. "c" is the reverse – $50 million for the country which cheats. And "d" is the $30 million each country earns when both countries break the rules. So, in this case, if Iran and Venezuela had just worked together, they'd have both gotten the better payoff – $40 million! But no, they both chose selfish behaviour, settling for dominant strategies that left them with $30 million each. While $30 million isn't bad; it's not $40 million. This shows how the "cooperate, cooperate" strategy profile Pareto dominates the "defect, defect" one.

In the following chapter, we explore another exceptional game, the "second-price sealed-bid auction," where there is also a dominant strategy equilibrium.

Chapter 5

Not the First But the Second Price: Auctions

You know the saying: "If all you have is a hammer, everything looks like a nail." Well, after diving into game theory, you might find yourself spotting strategic dilemmas just like many economists who've fallen under its spell. One reason game theory (and mathematical modelling in general) is so handy is because lots of seemingly unrelated situations share similar underlying structures. In the previous chapter, we talked about the Prisoner's Dilemma, which pops up in all sorts of scenarios where dominant and dominated strategies are at play. In this chapter, we're about to shift gears into the world of auctions using the toolkit of game theory. Theory of auctions is quite important for Economics in understanding pricing mechanisms.

Now, picture this: we're in London, at none other than the prestigious Christie's Auction House. It's 2023, and the London City Council has decided it simply *must* have a rare manuscript of Shakespeare's works. Enter Mr. John Smith, the council's representative, who's been sent to Christie's with strict instructions to bring home the prize. The council has crunched the numbers and set a hard cap of £200,000 for the manuscript – no exceptions. Mr. Smith was instructed that if he exceeds this budget, even by a single pound, he'll have to dip into his own pocket to cover the difference.

When he enters the auction room, Mr. Smith realizes that there are other eager bidders in the room. While each bidder knows their own limit, no one knows how much the others are willing to pay. It's like a high-stakes game of poker, except the cards are budgets, and nobody wants to fold too soon.

Let's first consider an ascending auction format. The auctioneer kicks things off by setting the starting bid at £100,000. The rules are simple: each participant can raise the bid in increments of £500. First, the participants eagerly raise bids as the budgets are not binding yet. But when the price hits £175,000, the air starts to thin. Mr. Smith, still safely under his budget cap, confidently raises the bid to £175,500. He looks around and realizes that no one else is willing to follow his lead. The auctioneer, ever the professional, calls out the familiar "going once, going twice, sold" (three times, just to be sure), and just like that, Mr. Smith secures the manuscript for £175,500. He walks back to his office in London feeling like a hero, having spent less than the city's £200,000 budget. But what really went down here?

Let's break it down. Say there were three bidders, including Mr. Smith. Suppose that their max limits were £150,000 and £175,000. Like Mr. Smith, they would face personal loss if they exceeded their limits. The auctioneer began at £100,000, and each participant had two options: raise the bid by £500 or sit tight. Naturally, at £100,000, everyone is more than happy to raise. So, if Mr. Smith hadn't jumped in, he would have lost the manuscript. But, if he were the only one to raise the bid to £100,500, he would have acquired the manuscript at a much lower price. If the other two could also raise the stakes, then again raising would ensure that Mr. Smith stayed in the game. At £100,000, raising the bid by £500 was the dominant strategy for Mr. Smith and for the other two participants.

As long as the bids stayed below £150,000, everyone kept bidding. But once the bid hit £150,000, the first participant hit their limit. For them, raising the bid further would mean a loss, so they bowed out. When the bid climbed to £175,000, the second participant waved the white flag too, for the same reason. But Mr. Smith? He was still in the game, and raising the bid to £175,500 was a no-brainer – so he did it and walked away victorious. Even though the council was prepared to fork out a hefty £200,000, Mr. Smith only had to shell out £175,500, just enough to edge out the second-highest bidder.

SECOND PRICE

THE FIRST GAME THEORIST IN THE WORLD

WHAT I FOUND IN THE GARAGE!

INVENTED AUCTIONS...

ANYONE WANT TO RAISE!

THE FRAME IS NICE. THIS IS WORTH $1.

THE FIRST ART HISTORIAN IN THE WORLD

LOOK AT THE FRAME!

99 CENTS!

GOOD. THEY DO NOT KNOW ART.

REALIZED THE IMPORTANCE OF THE SECOND PRICE!

$1

SELLING, SELLING, SOLD!

IT IS SUFFICIENT TO OFFER A SECOND PRICE!

WHEN IT WAS REALIZED THAT THE SECOND PRICE WINS IN OPEN AUCTIONS, A LOGICAL ALTERNATIVE TO HOLDING AN OPEN AUCTION WAS TO CONDUCT A SEALED-BID AUCTION WHERE THE HIGHEST BIDDER PAYS THE SECOND-HIGHEST PRICE. THIS SEALED-BID METHOD WAS FIRST USED BY GOETHE IN 1797 TO SELL A BOOK HE HAD WRITTEN. HOWEVER, THE METHOD DID NOT BECOME WIDELY USED IN THE NINETEENTH CENTURY. IT WAS ONLY IN 1893 THAT THIS AUCTION METHOD BEGAN TO BE WIDELY USED BY STAMP COLLECTORS. IT WAS COLUMBIA UNIVERSITY'S WILLIAM VICKREY WHO FIRST SHOWED IN 1961 THAT THIS METHOD IS THEORETICALLY IDENTICAL TO AN OPEN AUCTION. THIS IS WHY THE METHOD IS ALSO KNOWN AS THE VICKREY AUCTION.

Let's have a second look from the auctioneer's perspective.

An auctioneer who comprehends the workings of the auction process can pretty much guess how things will play out. The manuscript will most likely go to the person who values it the most, but they'll probably end up paying just a smidge above the second-highest bidder's offer. Then, the auctioneer might as well design an auction based on this outcome.

Take the "second-price sealed-bid auction." Here's how it works: instead of calling out bids like in an open auction; every buyer secretly writes down their bid and seals it in an envelope. The auctioneer then awards the prize to the highest bidder but requires the bidder to pay the second-highest bid. In our example, the bidders submit £150,000, £175,000, and £200,000. The manuscript goes to the £200,000 bidder, but they only pay £175,000, much to their pleasant surprise. If the auctioneer knew the max limits of the participants, she would simply set the price to £200,000 and be done with it. However, the lack of this critical knowledge forces the hand of the auctioneer to choose a delicate design.

To see why participants would bid their true limits in a second-price auction, let's imagine you're bidding for yet another valuable item (because who doesn't love the thrill of an auction?). You're willing to fork over £200,000 for this treasure, but you have no idea how much the other participants are willing to pay. You've got three strategies: bid less than £200,000, bid exactly £200,000, or bid more than £200,000.

Now, bidding more than your limit is clearly a terrible idea, unless you're into financial disasters. You could either end up overpaying or lose the auction anyway, so that's a no-go. Bidding below £200,000? Well, that might cause you to lose out when you didn't have to.

Imagine you bid £175,000, but someone else values the item at £180,000 – you'd lose, all because you didn't go for your true limit. So, the dominant strategy is to bid exactly £200,000, your max value. This logic applies to everyone else in the game, meaning their best bet is also to bid on what they're truly willing to pay.

Now, let's revisit our example where the participants' valuations are £150,000, £175,000, and £200,000. The results in both the open auction and the second-price auction look similar. The person willing to pay £200,000 wins, and they'll only pay almost the second-highest bid – £175,000. The real difference between the two auction types is the info the auctioneer collects.

In an open auction, all the auctioneer really knows is that the highest bidder is at least willing to go up to £175,500. But in a second-price auction, the auctioneer learns exactly what everyone was willing to pay. If gathering this kind of information is valuable for whatever reason, then a second-price auction might just be the better choice.

A month later, Mr. Smith is meeting up with an old university buddy, Mark. They haven't seen each other in ages. So, after the usual "how've you been?" and almost polishing off their second cup of tea, Mr. Smith starts sharing a story about a recent experience with auctions. He enthusiastically explains how these auctions work, especially the sealed-bid system where the person running the show is able to screen the max limits of the bidders. Mark, who works for the Ministry of Education, finds this fascinating because the ministry is about to open bids for a new school project. Construction companies will submit their offers, and the ministry will pick the one that promises to build the school for the least cost. As they chat, it dawns on both: government tenders and auctions aren't all that different after all – they're basically the same strategic dance!

Back at his work, Mark gets ready for the big day, and sure enough, the school construction bidding kicks off. Three companies are competing, all promising to build the same project with the same high-quality materials. The only difference is their price tags. None of the companies knows what the others' cost levels are. Suppose that the Ministry of Education just wants to get the job done at the lowest price and favours no company over the other. To keep it fair, they decide to use a sealed-bid, second-price auction.

Of course, government tenders in real life are rarely this straightforward. There are always extra layers of drama we can't capture in this simplified story. For starters, government agencies are not always focused on saving money but could be willing to spend more money if they hope to get a higher quality. Sometimes, behind-the-scenes deals might tip the scales, and the company that doesn't have the lowest bid could still win the contract. Or maybe the companies find ways to collude with each other and agree to share the pie – one gets this project, the other gets the next one, and everyone hikes up their prices. But we will leave these more dramatic scenarios to more advanced modelling and stick with our simple, clean version for now.

So, in this kind of auction, each company writes down their price to build the school and slips it into a sealed envelope, along with their company details. The Ministry opens them one by one and picks the lowest bid. If there's a tie for the lowest bid, the Ministry throws the names of the lowest bidders into a hat and randomly picks a winner. However, since it's a second-price auction, the lucky winner only needs to match the second-lowest bid. Assuming that no extra budget requests are allowed during construction, the winner can walk away with a sweet profit as long as it manages to build the project under budget. But if they overshoot, they eat the loss. Each company's minimum bid is basically the actual cost of the project or the lowest price that still lets them make a minimally acceptable profit.

In a way, this procurement auction game is like the reverse of the earlier auction for the manuscript. No company in their right mind would bid below their actual cost. No matter what the others bid, they face two possible outcomes: win the contract and build the school with the budget they've been given or lose the auction and go home empty-handed. If they bid too low, they might win but end up in the red. If they bid too high, they risk losing to a more competitive company. So, the smartest move for all three companies is to bid exactly what it costs them to build the school. It's an "honest" strategy, and in this game, honesty really is the best policy.

******

In the following chapter, we talk about another game, which can be solved with "iterated dominance" this time, and it is called the "Beauty Contest" game.

Chapter 6

A Guessing Game: Who Will Win the Beauty Contest?

Back in the 1930s, some British newspapers had beauty contests where people had to guess which woman from a set of photos would be voted the most beautiful. If you guessed right, you could win a prize. The renowned British economist John Maynard Keynes found these contests fascinating, and in his groundbreaking work, *The General Theory of Employment, Interest, and Money*, he compared financial investing to these very contests. According to Keynes, investors don't necessarily pick assets based on their actual value but rather on what they *think* others will find popular. And it doesn't stop there – some investors take it a step further, trying to predict what others will think *others* will find popular. In fact, some investors go further and try to predict what others will predict about what others will predict and so on.

As Keynes pointed out, when everyone is busy trying to guess what the other person is thinking, strategic uncertainty kicks in and so the outcome becomes hard to predict. We dive deeper into this later. In some cases where the players are sophisticated enough, all this guessing leads to a single, logical point. One game that demonstrates this concept perfectly and helps explain Keynes's comparison between investing and beauty contests is called the "guessing game."

THE WILLENDORF VENUS, MADE 32,000 YEARS AGO, IS THE FIRST DISCOVERED VENUS STATUE. THESE VENUS STATUES, WHICH WERE VERY POPULAR DURING THE PALEOLITHIC ERA, SHOW THAT THE AESTHETIC AND BEAUTY STANDARDS OF THAT TIME WERE DIFFERENT FROM TODAY'S. IF THERE HAD BEEN BEAUTY CONTESTS BACK THEN, WHERE PRIZES WERE GIVEN TO THOSE WHO PREDICTED WHO THE PUBLIC WOULD FIND MOST BEAUTIFUL, THOSE RESEMBLING THE VENUS STATUES WOULD HAVE BEEN CHOSEN. IN HIS 1936 BOOK "THE GENERAL THEORY OF EMPLOYMENT, INTEREST, AND MONEY," JOHN MAYNARD KEYNES ARGUED THAT WHEN INVESTORS CHOOSE WHICH FINANCIAL INSTRUMENTS – LIKE STOCKS, BONDS, OR EVEN HOUSES – TO INVEST IN, THEY ACT JUST LIKE IN BEAUTY CONTESTS, FOCUSING ON POPULAR INVESTMENTS.

The Guessing Game: This is a game where multiple players each choose a number between 0 and 100 (inclusive), and the player who picks the number closest to the average of all chosen numbers multiplied by some number p wins. The multiplier p can be any number between 0 and 1, but 2/3 is most used.[1]

According to this game, each player will pick a number between 0 and 100 without telling other players. Then, all numbers will be collected and the player who picked the number closest to two-thirds of the average wins the game. Whenever we run this game with students in a classroom, we observe a wild variety of guesses.

Now, it's your turn! If readers of this book were to pick a number between 0 and 100 and send it to us, what number would you pick? Remember, the

---

[1] Nagel, R. "Unraveling in guessing games: An experimental study." *The American Economic Review* 85, no. 5 (1995): 1313–1326.

goal is to choose a number closest to two-thirds of the average. Go ahead, take a moment to think about it before we move on!

******

It is possible to analyze the guessing game using the solution concepts dominant and dominated strategies – but this time, with a little twist. We're going to do this iteratively! First, we'll toss out all the dominated strategies for all players. Then, we'll take a second pass, focusing on the strategies that remain and weeding out any new dominated strategies. Rinse and repeat! We'll keep removing dominated strategies round by round until there's only one left standing, if any. This process is known as iterated elimination of strictly dominated strategies (or simply as iterative dominance). Iterative dominance often does not lead to a single strategy profile, but in this game it does.

In the application of this game, it is often assumed that all players are perfectly rational, and it is commonly known among them. These two assumptions are common in game theory. However, we will talk about other ways of modelling in the following.

To make things more concrete, imagine three friends – Alice, Ben, and Chloe – are playing the game, each trying to guess the average of the other two's chosen numbers. Is there a dominated strategy for Alice? Let's test it with the number 10. For Alice to rationalize choosing 10, the average of Ben and Chloe's numbers would need to be 15. If Ben goes with 20 and Chloe picks 10, then Alice's choice of 10 is the best reply. So, 10 is not a dominated strategy – it can work out just fine depending on what Ben and Chloe do.

But now try a larger number, like 80. For 80 to make sense, the average of Ben and Chloe's numbers would have to be 120. But there's no way that's happening. Even if Ben and Chloe both pick the max number, 100, the average would still only be 100, and two-thirds of that is 66.7. So, 80 is way too high and can never be a good choice. In fact, we can now say with confidence that no number above 66.7 can ever make sense because no matter what numbers Ben and Chloe pick, two-thirds of their average will never exceed 66.7.

The same logic applies to Ben and Chloe. So, for all three players, any number above 66.7 is a dominated strategy and can be eliminated from the game. Now, we're left with numbers between 0 and 66.7. What's next? We go back to the drawing board, peel away more layers of dominated strategies, and keep narrowing down the options.

To get a clearer picture of the next step, let's break down why we can confidently toss out numbers greater than 66.7. It's simple: we assume that all three players – Alice, Ben, and Chloe – are smart enough to avoid unreasonably high numbers. Furthermore, all players know how smart the other players are. Alice knows that Ben and Chloe are rational and so would not pick a dominated strategy. Ben knows that Alice and Chloe are also rational, and Chloe knows the same about Alice and Ben. It's a mutual understanding that nobody is going to pick a number higher than 66.7.

The players can as well implement iterative dominance to not only eliminate dominated strategies for themselves but also make predictions of what other players do. So, all players eliminate the dominated strategies of their opponents.

In the second stage, looking at the game from Ben's point of view, is 30 a bad choice for him? For two-thirds of the average to be 30, Alice and Chloe's numbers would need to average out to 45. If, for example, Alice picks 50 and Chloe picks 40, Ben's choice of 30 would be perfect. So, 30 is not dominated. But what about 50? For 50 to be two-thirds of the average,

Alice and Chloe would need to average out to 75. But Ben knows that Alice and Chloe are way too clever to pick numbers higher than 66.7. So, 50 is now a dominated strategy. In fact, Ben can eliminate any number higher than 44.44 (since two-thirds of 66.67 is 44.44). The same goes for Alice and Chloe – they won't be picking anything over 44.44 either because they're all in this rational-thinking club.

Now, onto the third stage, with Chloe's perspective in mind. Chloe's figured out that 66.7 and numbers higher than 44.44 are off the table. Like Alice and Ben, she knows they're all rational and would avoid dominated strategies. Furthermore, she knows that Ben and Alice know all the players are rational too. So, Chloe can predict that they definitely won't pick any number over 44.44.

Would Chloe, for instance, pick 40? For two-thirds of the average to be 40, Ben and Alice's numbers would need to average out to 60. But Chloe knows that Ben and Alice aren't picking anything over 44.44. With this second-level reasoning, Chloe realizes that anything above 29.62 (since two-thirds of 44.44 is 29.62) is a dominated strategy.

And so, with each round of elimination, our players keep narrowing down the numbers, leaving only the most rational choices in the game.

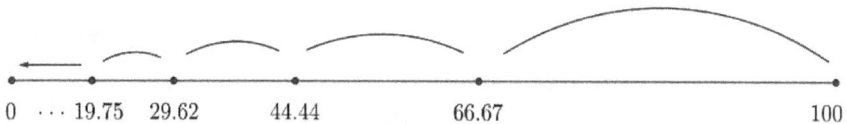

| 0 | $\cdots$ 19.75 | 29.62 | 44.44 | 66.67 | 100 |

But does the story end here? Not quite! As Alice, Ben, and Chloe are truly rational and they're all certain that the others are just as rational, they can keep this reasoning going and eliminate numbers all the way down to 0. Let's walk through why.

For any number greater than 0 to make sense, the other two players' average needs to be such that two-thirds of it equals the number chosen. If you keep multiplying 100 by two-thirds, the result keeps shrinking and shrinking, getting closer and closer to 0. So, with this infinite loop of rationality, every number greater than 0 is slowly but surely eliminated as a dominated strategy.

Now, let's see if 0 really holds up as a reasonable choice for all the players. Imagine Ben and Chloe both decide to pick 0. In that case, the average is 0, and two-thirds of 0 is still 0. Alice would look at that and say, "Well, if they're both picking 0, I guess I'll pick 0 too." And just like that, 0 becomes a perfectly rational choice for Alice. Since this same logic works for Ben and Chloe, we can say that 0 is a reasonable strategy for everyone involved.

Best Response: The choice that yields the highest payoff for a player, given their beliefs or knowledge about the choices and outcomes of other players.

Rationalizable Strategy: A strategy that is the best response for a player under at least one belief about what other players might do.

Just like many economists, we often have our students play the guessing game in our game theory classes. Now, you'd think after all that theory, they'd jump straight to choosing 0, right? Not quite! What we typically see is a wide range of different numbers. Some students just pick a random number between 0 and 100, while others choose a number closer to one-third of 100. When we look at these real-life results, it's clear that our beautifully crafted theoretical analysis doesn't always hold up in practice.

When the model and its tidy logic don't quite match up with what we see in the real world, it's time to question the assumptions behind the model. In our earlier analysis, we made two pretty big assumptions. First, we assumed that all players were rational, thus, fully capable of understanding the rules and making perfect calculations like some kind of human calculator. The second – and possibly the biggest stretch – was that everyone knew that everyone else was rational.

> **Common Knowledge:** A situation in which every player in a group knows a certain fact, every player knows that every other player knows this fact, and every player knows that every other player knows that every other player knows this fact, and so on.

In the world of behavioural game theory, there's a model that steps in when we loosen up those two assumptions: it's called Cognitive Hierarchy. Think of it as a more realistic take on how people actually behave in games like the guessing game. Instead of assuming everyone is rational, this model assumes that players employ different levels of strategic depths while thinking, and we can represent these levels of numbers using 0, 1, 2, and so on.

Level 0 represents people who play completely randomly without any strategic articulation. This is as if rolling a dice to make their choices. At Level 1, players assume everyone else is at Level 0, playing randomly. So, Level 1 players calculate the best response against the expected average of random numbers.

At Level 2, players are a bit more sophisticated. They believe that some players are at Level 0 (random players), while others are at Level 1 (thinking one step ahead). The Level 2 player then crunches the numbers, considers the mix of random guessers and overthinkers, and picks their strategy accordingly. Similarly, Level 3 players believe that everyone else is operating somewhere between Level 0 and Level 2, and they choose the best reply according to some expected mix of levels from 0 to 2. In general, players at Level k assume the rest of the crowd is playing anywhere between Level 0 and Level $k-1$, meaning they calculate their best strategy based on what they believe all the "less advanced" players are doing.

> **Cognitive Hierarchy Model:** A model, particularly used in behavioural economics experiments, where players choose strategies based on their mental levels, which may involve playing randomly or selecting a strategy that is the best response to the belief that others are playing randomly or choosing their best response to random play, and so on. It is an alternative to the standard model, where all players are assumed to be perfectly rational, and this is common knowledge.

In the quote we mentioned at the beginning of this chapter, Keynes also introduced a concept that fits right in with the Cognitive Hierarchy Model. Fast forward a few decades, and Nobel laureate Reinhard Selten, had a similar idea, suggesting that step-by-step reasoning would be a better way to analyze games. It was Colin Camerer and his colleagues, big names in behavioural economics, who took these ideas and ran with them in 2004, developing a statistical model to back it all up.[2]

The Cognitive Hierarchy Model is a lot more flexible than the rational choice model. This flexibility lets it explain real-world behaviours – whether in a classroom setting where students are playing games, or in carefully controlled laboratory experiments.

To make things a bit more concrete, let's revisit our friends Alice, Ben, and Chloe. But let's assume they're all operating at different levels of reasoning. Alice is at Level 0, Ben is at Level 1, and Chloe is at Level 2. Here's how that plays out:

Alice, operating at Level 0, doesn't give much thought to the game. She's not bothered by strategies or reasoning – she just randomly picks a number between 0 and 100. Maybe she's exhausted after a long day, or maybe she's

---

[2] Camerer, Colin F., Teck-Hua Ho, and Juin-Kuan Chong. "A cognitive hierarchy model of games." *Quarterly Journal of Economics*, 119, no. 3 (2004): 861–898.

just not that interested in guessing games right now. Whatever the reason, she picks the first number that pops into her head.

Now, let's turn our attention to Ben, who's reasoning at Level 1. Ben, in his mind, is the lone genius among the three, assuming that both Alice and Chloe are just picking numbers at random. Ben figures that he should choose two-thirds of the expected average of their random numbers. There are 101 numbers between 0 and 100 (yes, we're counting 0), and if every number is equally likely to be chosen, the probability of any one number being picked is 1/101. Then, the expected number that each of his opponents will pick is

$$(0 + 1 + 2 + \cdots + 100) / 101 = (100 * 101) / (2 * 101) = 50.$$

The average is 50. As the average of two 50's is still a 50, Ben figures out that his best reply is its best reply, 33.3.

Now, let's turn to Chloe, who's operating at Level 2. Chloe might be believing that both Alice and Ben are just picking random numbers, or they are reasoning at Level 1, which means they've settled on 33.3 after assuming everyone else is picking randomly. Or Chloe could believe that one of them is playing randomly while the other is stuck at 33.3. Let's assume that Chloe's beliefs are consistent with what we have assumed thus far. Therefore, Chloe believes that Alice is picking a random number (like 50, as the average random guess), while Ben assumes everyone else is playing randomly and picks 33.3. So, what does Chloe do? Well, she averages Alice's 50 and Ben's 33.3, getting 41.65. Then, she picks two-thirds of 41.65, which is 27.77.

So, based on the reasoning levels of our trio – Alice playing randomly, Ben sitting on 33.3, and Chloe calculating her way to 27.77 – we expect to see these numbers pop up in their game. If we observed a guessing game with three individuals where the results were something like 33.3, 27.77, and, say, 62 (from Alice's random guess), this would fit perfectly with the Cognitive Hierarchy Model we've been discussing.

Now, if we wanted to take this further and figure out the distribution of cognitive levels within a larger group, we could have a whole bunch of people playing this game over and over again. By collecting the results, we'd get a clearer idea of how these cognitive levels are spread out. In fact, in the article by Camerer, Ho, and Chong that we mentioned earlier, they show that the average cognitive level across many experiments is around 1.5. So, most people are somewhere between random guessing and thinking one step ahead.

******

In most game theory models, we like to assume that the players are all rational and, more importantly, that they all know that everyone else is too. While this assumption has been challenged by researchers in behavioural economics, it's still a helpful benchmark.

For games like the guessing game, this assumption lets us reach a clear, definitive conclusion. However, in most of the more interesting and messy situations, this assumption isn't enough by itself to lead us to a single outcome. Often, the result depends on how we model the players' expectations or, more precisely, in what ways those expectations are coordinated. This brings us to one of the most important ideas in game theory: equilibrium. In the following chapter, we dive into the most important and common equilibrium notion: the Nash equilibrium.

Chapter 7

Nash Equilibrium: Where Will the Lovers Meet?

One of the standout films from a remarkably productive year in Hollywood, 1999, was *The Matrix*. Hidden in this film is a scene that brilliantly illustrates a concept straight out of game theory: the idea of a self-fulfilling prophecy. Remember that part where Neo visits the Oracle to find out if he's truly "The One"? Before his visit, he does not believe in oracles or prophecies. When he enters the room of the Oracle, a calm woman baking cookies in her kitchen greets him. She tells him right away that "Don't worry about the vase."

Neo, turns around to locate a vase while murmuring "What vase?" and knocks over a vase on the table, which shatters into pieces. While Neo scrambles to clean up, the Oracle simply says, "That vase." Mind blown, Neo asks, "How did you know?" The Oracle replies, "What's really going to bake your noodle later on is that would you still have broken it if I hadn't said anything?"

In economics, a **self-fulfilling prophecy** occurs when decision-makers' beliefs about what others will do lead everyone to make choices that confirm those beliefs. Imagine a rumour spreads that a bank is about to fail. If enough people believe this and rush to withdraw their money, they might actually cause the bank to run out of cash – making the rumour come true, even if it wasn't before![1]

This idea of self-fulfilling prophecy helps us understand Nash equilibrium, one of the cornerstones of game theory. But before diving into the details, let's think about this: imagine a group of players getting ready to play a strategic game. They gather in a room, and an oracle walks in and announces what strategy each player will choose. The players then go off to make their decisions.

Now, each player thinks, "If everyone else believes the prophecy and plays the strategy the oracle said they would, is it in my best interest to follow the prophecy?" If the strategy predicted for a player is better than all other strategies against what everyone else is doing, then we can call this strategy the player's best response. In a Nash equilibrium, every player's strategy is the best response to the strategies chosen by the other players. In a two-player game, this means that both players play best responses against each other's strategies. In this setup, no player can improve their outcome by changing their strategy – any deviation would only hurt them in the end.

The oracle in our story isn't really predicting the future here, but she knows a thing or two about game theory. Specifically, she knows that prophecies predicting a Nash equilibrium could self-fulfil if she manages to coordinate the expectations of the players.

In short, a Nash equilibrium is a strategy profile where no player can gain by unilaterally switching strategies. Everyone is playing the best they can, given what everyone else is doing. At this point, it's worth noting that while

---

[1] For a classical reference about the application of the self-fulfilling prophecies to banking crises, see the works of Diamond, D. W. and Dybvig, P. H. "Bank runs, deposit insurance, and liquidity." *Journal of Political Economy*, 91, no. 3 (1983): 401–419.

some games have just one Nash equilibrium, others have multiple equilibria. When there are multiple Nash equilibria, it's a bit like that circular thinking we saw with the self-fulfilling prophecy: if players expect a certain outcome, they'll often act in ways that will make it happen.

One of the most famous examples of a game with multiple Nash equilibria is the Battle of the Sexes, a two-player game that we discuss in the following.

7.1. Battle of the Sexes

O. Henry's classic 1905 short story *The Gift of the Magi* perfectly illustrates how lack of coordination can lead to some unfortunate outcomes. It's a Christmas story of a couple, Della and Jim Magi, who love each other deeply but must live on little income. Determined to surprise each other with a Christmas gift, they each make a huge sacrifice. Della sells her beautiful hair to buy Jim a fine chain for his watch, while Jim sells his prized watch to buy combs for Della's hair. Each ends up with a thoughtful gift, but neither will have a practical use for it!

Now, imagine if Della and Jim had coordinated a bit better. Maybe they could have flipped a coin to decide who would sacrifice. For instance, they could decide that it is Della who can make a sacrifice this time. This would be better for Jim and much less for Della, but it would still be better than no coordination.

Coordination is a core theme in The Battle of the Sexes, a game that explores the balance between cooperation and conflict.

In our version of the story, let's meet Jane and John. These two are the kind of couple that love spending time together so much so that it does not matter what they do if they are not together. However, they each have their own idea of what a perfect evening looks like. John prefers a cosy pub that brews its own beer (but doesn't serve coffee or tea), while Jane is all about a café that's famous for its coffee and tea (but no alcohol).

Recently, they had a bit of an argument and aren't currently speaking to each other. But next Friday is their anniversary; so, it's the perfect chance to make up! Both Jane and John plan to go out that night. If they happen to go to the same spot, they will have a chance to patch things up.

		Jane	
		Pub	Café
John	Pub	(3,1)	(0,0)
	Café	(0,0)	(1,3)

Here's how it works: John gets 3 units of utility if he and Jane meet at his beloved pub, and 1 unit if they meet at the café she likes. Jane, meanwhile, gets 3 units if they meet at the café and 1 unit if they end up at the pub. If they go to different places, it's a zero for both. The first number in the table shows John's payoff, while the second shows Jane's.

Now, imagine the worst-case scenario: John heads to the café, thinking he'll meet Jane there, while Jane goes to the pub, hoping to find John. They miss each other completely and spend the entire evening running back and forth between the pub and café, never quite meeting up. Let's just hope they don't wear themselves out from all that running.

Another bad scenario is when John goes to his pub, and Jane goes to her café. Sure, they're both at their favourite spots, but without each other's company, neither is happy.

The remaining are better options. They both go to the pub, which makes John a bit happier (since it's his favourite), or they both go to the café, which leaves Jane with a bigger smile. Either way, they at least get to spend time together.

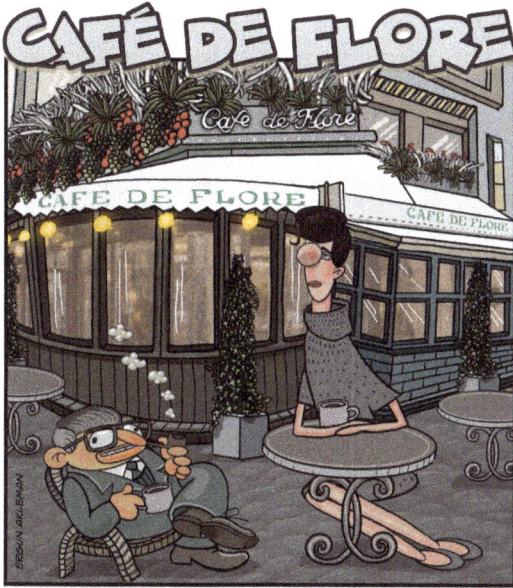

IN THE 1950s, ALL YOU HAD TO DO TO SEE JEAN-PAUL SARTRE AND SIMONE DE BEAUVOIR WAS TO GO TO CAFÉ DE FLORE. THE TWO PHILOSOPHERS KNEW THEY WOULD FIND EACH OTHER THERE, EVEN IF THEY HAD A FIGHT. CAFÉ DE FLORE IS ONE OF THE OLDEST COFFEEHOUSES IN PARIS. AMONG ITS REGULAR PATRONS WERE NOT ONLY JEAN-PAUL SARTRE AND SIMONE DE BEAUVOIR BUT ALSO ALBERT CAMUS, PABLO PICASSO, GEORGES BATAILLE, ROBERT DESNOS, LÉON-PAUL FARGUE, AND RAYMOND QUENEAU. THESE DAYS, YOU'RE LIKELY TO ONLY SEE OTHER TOURISTS THERE. THEREFORE, IF YOU LOSE EACH OTHER AS TOURISTS IN PARIS, ONE OF THE BEST PLACES TO REUNITE IS CAFÉ DE FLORE.

Note that there's no clear dominant strategy here. It is not the case that one person can simply pick a strategy that guarantees the best outcome no matter what. What we do have are best responses – strategies that make sense based on what the other person is likely to do.

If Jane decides to go to the café, the best thing John can do is follow her to the café. Likewise, if Jane heads to the pub, John's best move is to tag along and join her there. It's the same the other way around: if John chooses the café, Jane's best response is to go to the café, and if John chooses the pub, Jane's best response is to hit the pub.

In this game, it's clear that John and Jane heading to different spots isn't a great strategy – neither of them gets to enjoy the evening if they end up at different places. But when they head to the same spot, whether it's the café or the pub, they're making the best response to each other's strategy. When each player's move is the best response to the other's, we have a Nash equilibrium.

In the Battle of the Sexes, there are at least two Nash equilibria: one where they both head to the café and one where they both go to the pub.

> **Multiple Equilibria:** The case that occurs when a game has more than one equilibrium point. In such instances, the outcome of the game is determined not only by the game's defining variables but also by which beliefs and strategies the players coordinate on.

Each Nash equilibrium rests on a static version of strategic stability – kind of like a perfectly balanced seesaw. Let's take the equilibrium where John and Jane both head to the café. In this scenario, they each believe the other is going to the café, and they both know that if one of them tries to do something else, say if John goes to the pub, he will lose out because he won't get to meet Jane. The same goes for the equilibrium with pub and Jane. If she suddenly decides to swap her cosy café for the pub, she'll find herself alone. In any Nash equilibrium, players stick to their strategy because they know it's their best option, given what the others are doing. If they tried to do something different, they'd end up worse off. That's why Nash equilibria are strategically stable – it is like being stuck in a spot where no one wants to leave because they know they won't find anything better.

Here's a metaphor from physics to understand strategic stability: imagine the strategy profiles in a game as different stops that the players can reach, like stations on a subway line. To move from one stop (a strategy profile) to another, one player has to decide to make the jump. But when the players are sitting happily at a Nash equilibrium stop, no one wants to get up and move because they know the next stop isn't as good. Once everyone is there, they're comfortable. This stop is stable as there is no strategic movement to another stop.

In games like the Battle of the Sexes, the presence of multiple Nash equilibria makes it harder to predict the outcome. Will they end up at the café or the pub? The rules and payoffs alone can't tell us that. Other factors – like a common event or a little communication – might be needed to nudge them in one direction. Maybe a well-timed text, "Hey, meet me at the pub!" could do the trick, or maybe they'll both spot a sign for happy hour at the café and decide to meet there instead.

Let's return to John and Jane's Friday night dilemma. John's close buddy Tom knows how upset John has been ever since their argument and is scratching his head, trying to figure out how to help. Now, Tom could play the role of the oracle we mentioned earlier and swoop in to resolve the dilemma. Tom sends a message to both, casually mentioning that there's a great band performing at John's favourite pub this Friday. Actually, there is no such band playing, and John and Jane, both know it. But they also know that Tom is on their side and just wants them to meet.

After receiving the message, Jane might think, "Hmm, maybe John's planning to head to the pub as a surprise for our anniversary. After all, he probably thinks I'll go there for the same reason." In this case, Jane would decide to head to the pub. Meanwhile, John is thinking the exact same thing: "Maybe Jane's going to the pub because she expects me to show up." After Tom's message, heading to the pub becomes an easy choice for both John and Jane. Tom's little white lie has successfully nudged them towards the Nash equilibrium where they both meet up at the pub for a happy reunion.

Of course, we could flip the script and imagine a different outcome – one where the Nash equilibrium leads them to the café. This time, instead of Tom, it's Jane's close friend Sarah who jumps into action. She sends a message to both John and Jane, telling them about a new poetry reading event happening at the café. Just like Tom's message, Sarah's well-intentioned intervention could be enough to convince John and Jane that the café is the place to be.

7.2. Focal Points

Sometimes, reaching a Nash equilibrium or choosing between multiple equilibria doesn't rely on well-meaning oracles like Tom or Sarah but on cultural norms and expectations. Take John and Jane, for example. If they live in a more traditional society, where men are expected to take initiative, they might assume it is John who is supposed to surprise Jane. And for John to pull off his surprise, Jane would need to play it cool and go to the café – just like she would if she wasn't expecting anything special. Knowing this expectation, John might predict that Jane will head to the café, figuring it's up to him to make the surprise. Meanwhile, Jane, aware of the tradition, goes to the café, expecting John to show up as a romantic gesture.

> A **focal point** is a Nash equilibrium where players coordinate their strategies without needing to talk things out – often thanks to cultural or historical clues. For instance, if you asked, "When and where should we meet in London?" without giving people a chance to communicate, they might all answer, "At noon at Trafalgar Square." A focal point is often called a Schelling point.

These cultural codes act like a kind of unspoken GPS that helps players navigate towards one of the multiple Nash equilibria. Schelling, who won a Nobel Prize for his work, gave us the idea of local focal points – places or times that help people coordinate without needing to say a word. For example, a couple trying to meet up in New York without communicating might instinctively choose Grand Central Station, and odds are they would choose noon as the time. Similarly, a couple in London might pick Trafalgar Square at noon.

But these local focal points don't always have to be physical meeting spots. In John and Jane's case, the idea that it's John's job to make the big surprise effort could itself be a focal point. Likewise, there could be an expectation that in romantic relationships, it's the guy who should approach the woman first, giving the woman a chance to respond. These norms can be so strong that if a guy is dragging his feet on making the move, the woman might not think that he does not know the norms but instead, she might think that "He's just not that into me."

Chapter 8

Fight to the End: From Bertrand Equilibrium to War of Attrition

James wanted to surprise his spouse with the latest "Reverse" sports shoes; so, he headed to the busiest shopping street in town. This street was home to two shoe shops, owned by Alice and Ben, who had been selling shoes and bags to the same group of customers for years. Whenever the latest shoe trend hit, the neighbourhood's young people would rush to these two shops. Some would walk out with a shiny new pair, while others just wished they could. Now, Alice and Ben weren't big fans of haggling, and to make this very clear, they both had large, no-nonsense signs at the front of their shops: "No Haggling."

As James visited both stores to check out the Reverse shoes, he discovered that Ben's shop had the shoes priced at £150, while Alice was selling them for £160. "It's better not to waste £10," he thought, and off he went to buy the shoes from Ben. During the day, Alice was noting a trend: quite a few customers like James would come in, check the shoes and the prices, and then disappear, never to return. She began to suspect something was up. She knew only two things could be happening – either the price was a bit too high for some, so they decided not to buy any shoes at all, or her customers had found a better deal at Ben's. She sent her assistant to check out Ben's prices.

By evening, her assistant came back with the news: Ben's shop was offering the shoes for £150. "Ah, that's why!" thought Alice. Not one to be outdone, she closed shop and slashed the price to £140 for the next day.

The following morning, the street was buzzing with activity. Sarah, a university student who had been eagerly waiting for the new Reverse shoes, headed to the street with £140 in her pocket. She hoped that this much money was just enough to grab the shoes and still have enough left for a coffee at the campus café. When she saw the £140 price at Alice's shop, she was happy that she could afford the shoes but could use a bit cheaper price so that she could get a coffee later. She figured she'd check out Ben's shop too, just in case. Seeing Ben's price of £150, Sarah sighed, "No coffee today, I guess," and went back to Alice's shop for the purchase.

Alice was feeling great about her sales – finally, a busy day! But by the evening, it was Ben's turn to scratch his head. His shop had been unusually quiet all day, with customers coming in, glancing at the price, and walking out. He decided to take a page from Alice's book and sent his own assistant to check the competition. When he found out that Alice had dropped her price to £140, Ben had a flashback to that university student muttering about coffee before leaving his shop. "Aha! So that's what that was about!" he realized. There was only one thing to do – lower his price!

The next day, Ben dropped his price to £130. Once again, it was Alice's turn to look behind the customers leaving her shop. She decided she wasn't going down without a fight. By evening, she had cut her price to £120. Not to be outdone, Ben responded the following day by dropping his price to £110. This back-and-forth price slashing couldn't go on forever, of course. Eventually, both Alice and Ben would hit a point, where lowering the price any further would mean selling the shoes at a loss. How much longer this war of attrition would continue depended entirely on how low they were willing to go before one of them called it quits.

Let's assume Alice and Ben are playing on a level field. They both work with the same suppliers, pay the same rent, and have one trusty assistant each, both earning minimum wage. With similar customer profiles, it turns out the amount of money they need to keep their shops afloat is almost identical. The cost of these brand-new Reverse shoes from the wholesaler? £90 a pair. To cover their other expenses, they need to add at least £10 on top, so their absolute minimum selling price is £100.

One day, when Alice finds out that Ben has priced his shoes at £110, she lets out a big sigh and lowers her price to £100, muttering, "No profit on this one, but at least I won't lose customers." The next morning, Ben notices he's losing customers again and grumbles, "Fine, fine!" and drops his price to £100 too.

Fast-forward a week, and every customer strolling through the shops discovers the same thing – both stores are selling the Reverse shoes for £100. Customer looking for these shoes just pick the shop that is more conveniently on their way. So, around half of them go to Alice's shop and the others choose Ben's. Meanwhile, Alice and Ben note that things have settled down. Sales are about half of what they were during the best days of the chaotic price war. With the storm behind them, they can focus on their regular routines. This balanced situation continues, day after day, until the next big fashion wave arrives and sends them back into the competition.

Alice and Ben's battle is a textbook example of what companies face all over the world when they sell the same (or very similar) products to the same customers. This kind of price-cutting battle is known as Bertrand competition, named after Joseph Bertrand, a French mathematician who modelled this price-cutting game way back in the 1880s – long before John Nash proved his result about Nash equilibria. Bertrand figured out the Nash equilibrium for this situation, though surely, he didn't call it that at the time. In short, when both Alice and Ben end up selling their shoes at £100, they've reached an equilibrium point in their price war, one that Bertrand would have predicted over a century ago.

> **Bertrand Competition:** A game in which two firms selling the same product to the same type of buyers in the same market compete by setting prices simultaneously. If the firms have the same production costs, the Nash equilibrium price in this game equals the cost. This is because if all firms are expected to choose a price higher than cost, any firm can slightly lower its price to capture the entire market.

When two shops, like Alice and Ben's, have the same production or sales costs and both decide on prices at the same time, the price battle tends to have just one predictable outcome. Eventually, both shops lower their prices to the point where they're not making any profit on each sale. When customers spot identical prices in both stores, they'll choose whichever shop is closer or maybe the one with the comfier seating. The demand gets split between the two shops. However, if one of them has a slight cost advantage (maybe Ben gets a better deal on rent), the price war ends with the lower-cost shop winning, while the other realizes it can't keep cutting prices and waves the white flag.

Now, what if Alice and Ben could trust each other? They could agree to fix their prices at £150 and promise each other not to cut the price down. However, trust can be hard to establish. Without it, they're stuck in a scenario much like the Prisoner's Dilemma from our earlier OPEC example. Let's say they agree to keep prices at £150. But the next day, Alice could decide to play sneaky and drop her price to £140. She could sell shoes to all customers while Ben has a much lower demand. Furthermore, it would be more profitable for Alice to drop the price if she expects Ben to drop as well. This way at least she can get some of the customers to make a decent number of sales. Therefore, lowering the price is again the dominant strategy.

Situations like Bertrand competition pop up in all sorts of contexts and not just about price wars. Take political competition, for example. As elections approach, two or more political parties often get caught in a race of electoral platforms. One party pledges to raise pensions, while the other could be promising to cap energy bills. One party announces plans for investments in public infrastructure in swing cities or states, and the other could talk about public housing. The competition could also take a darker turn. One party leader's old recording, where he makes racist comments, might surface hit the media, while another's corruption scandal resurfaces. This back-and-forth "war of attrition" escalates all the way up to election day.

By the time voters head to the voting booths, the once-distinct parties may look nearly identical, at least to the undecided voters who've been caught in the crossfire. The election then becomes a contest of who's managed to stay cleaner and which party has a bigger, more loyal voter base.

Downsian Competition: A game where two political parties or candidates simultaneously choose policy proposals to win an election, with voters selecting the party or candidate whose policies are closest to their preferences. When voters' preferences can be ranked on a single dimension, such as a left-right ideological spectrum, the game's Nash equilibrium has both candidates choosing the policy preferred by the median voter.

Situations like wars of attrition show up in some of the more intense chapters of modern history, especially in civil wars. These conflicts often pit the state's official military and police against an illegal armed group. Since the state usually holds the power advantage, these groups don't go for open warfare. Instead, they lean into guerrilla tactics and terrorism, making life difficult for their more powerful rivals. When it is difficult for the parties to make compromises in a process of negotiations, these wars can drag on for years, causing destruction on both sides.

Eventually, most conflicts end in one way or another. Maybe the armed group shifts to non-violent strategies, like in the Northern Ireland–England situation in 1994. Or perhaps they manage to create a brand-new state – take South Sudan in 2011, for example. And sometimes, they sign a peace agreement, like in Colombia in 2016.

In war of attrition games, there's typically only one Nash equilibrium, even though the exact situation might differ. Both sides will push each other to their limits. If both sides have the same attrition costs – the same amount of resources to burn through – they'll keep fighting until they're equally worn down. But if one side has a clear advantage (more money, resources, or lower costs), the advantageous side wins.

8.1. The Hotelling Game

The Hotelling Game is used for competition among firms, where firms differentiate from each other according not to their qualities but rather to consumers' heterogeneous personal preferences over the firms. This kind of competition is often called horizontal competition. Even though the name Hotelling Game sounds like a battle between hotels over the best beachfront property, these games are named after economist Harold Hotelling, who first provided a mathematical analysis of such games.

Now, let's imagine a market where all the consumers live along a line. Each consumer can be described by their position on this line, which stretches from 0 to 1. For example, a consumer of type 0.3 lives at that exact spot on the line. Consumers are evenly spread along this line, meaning that the group between 0 and 0.1 makes up the same percentage (10%) as the group between 0.9 and 1.

Now, consider two producers who are about to open shops along this line, trying to attract as many customers as possible. After the shops open, let's assume that both producers charge the same price for their products. In this situation, each consumer will obviously go to the closest shop. For example, let's say one shop sets up at 0.25, and the other opens at 0.75. A consumer at 0.3 is only 0.05 units away from the first shop and 0.45 units away from the second. So, she would choose the shop at 0.25.

Knowing this, the producers will try to position their shops in ways that appeal to the most customers. The only Nash equilibrium (the point where no one has any reason to change their strategy) in this game is for both shops to set up at the exact middle, 0.5. Imagine one shop is expected to open at 0.6. The other firm can just pick 0.59 and grab all the customers from 0 to 0.59 – that's 59% of the market! Do we have a Nash equilibrium where there is one shop at 0.6 and the other at 0.59? No! The shop at 0.6 might choose 0.58 expecting to get the majority of the market. If one of the shops is expected to open at 0.5, there is no other strategy for the other shop except to open also at 0.5 and accept the fact that it cannot appeal to more than half of the market.

This game has various applications. For instance, if you think of the consumers as voters, the firms as political parties, and their locations as ideologies on the left-right spectrum, you've got yourself the Downsian political competition game that we briefly discussed just above. Politicians, like the firms here, will gravitate towards the middle to win as many votes as possible.

In many situations, the power of Nash equilibrium in the analysis of static interactions is rather limited. For instance, when interactions play out over time and players can observe each other's strategies and adjust, dynamic models from game theory become more useful, and for these models, we often need tools other than Nash equilibrium. In later chapters, we introduce these tools and talk about various applications.

Chapter 9

The Power of Unpredictability: Matching Pennies and Tax Evasion

In game theory, a popular and simple game called Matching Pennies helps illustrate probabilistic strategies between two players. Imagine two kids named Anna and Bob, each have a penny. They must simultaneously decide whether to show the heads or tails side of their penny to the other player. The outcome of the game depends on how their choices matchup: if both players choose the same side (both show heads or both show tails), then Anna wins. If the players choose different sides (one shows heads and the other shows tails), then Bob wins.

The game is structured so that both players have conflicting objectives. Anna wants to align their choice with Bob, but Bob wants the choices to differ. The game is a zero-sum game, where one player's gain is exactly the other player's loss.

		Bob	
		Heads	Tails
Anna	Heads	(1, −1)	(−1,1)
	Tails	(−1,1)	(1, −1)

If players chose pure strategies, they would choose one option consistently (either heads or tails). However, if either player consistently picks one option (e.g., always choosing heads), the other player can easily exploit this by choosing the opposite (or the same) to guarantee a win every time. In this game, you do not want to be predictable. To avoid this, players must use mixed strategies, where they randomize their choices. When a player uses mixed strategies, it becomes impossible to fully predict the moves of this player. This way a player can avoid being systematically beaten.

In this game, the only way to keep each of the players from consistently losing is to uniformly randomize their decisions. Anna and Bob will each choose heads or tails with a 50–50 probability, making it impossible for the other to predict their move reliably.

In the mixed-strategy Nash equilibrium, each player randomizes their choices, selecting heads or tails with equal probabilities. If Anna were to choose heads or tails more often, Bob could adjust his strategy to exploit Anna's bias. To avoid being predictable, Anna chooses heads and tails with a 50% probability for each. Likewise, if Bob chooses heads or tails with unequal probability, Anna can adjust her strategy to consistently win. To make sure that Anna cannot predict his moves, Bob also chooses heads and tails with a 50% probability for each.

To see that this is indeed a Nash equilibrium, note that no player can improve their expected payoff by unilaterally changing their strategy. Here's why the 50–50 randomization is stable for both players: Anna knows that Bob is randomizing with a 50–50 probability. Therefore, playing heads or tails yields the same expected payoff of 0. If Anna plays heads, with 0.5 probability she gets 1 and with the remaining probability she gets −1. The expected payoff is $0.5 * (-1) + 0.5 * 1 = 0$. The same calculation holds for choosing tails as well. Hence, Anna is completely indifferent between choosing these two strategies. Any choice of probabilities between heads and tails would yield the same payoff, and Anna cannot improve upon the Nash equilibrium strategy of 50–50 probability. Similarly, Bob knows that Anna is also randomizing with equal probability and so there is no way to improve. This shows that 50–50 probabilities are best responses to each other and so they constitute a Nash equilibrium.

9.1. The Tax Evasion Game

Now, let's consider a different scenario – tax evasion between a government agency and the notorious criminal Alec. The government suspects that Alec has committed many crimes as a crime boss but the only crime that the government can find some credible evidence of is tax evasion. Alec understands that he is a person of interest and therefore plans his illegal acts carefully. However, there is no perfect cover-up when it comes to crime. There could always be one loose end that could bring his demise. Therefore, every crime is a risk, especially tax evasion. The tax authority, the most rigorous government agency of all, can find any tax evasion if it allocates enough resources to monitoring. Despite the risk, paying tax is still costly, and Alec would avoid it if he knew the government were looking away.

In this game, Alec can either evade taxes by underreporting their income to pay less tax or comply by paying the full amount of taxes honestly. Without observing Alec's decision, the government can either choose to audit Alec by checking his tax returns and penalize any evasion or not audit.

The tax evasion game is similar to Matching Pennies in the sense that both players have conflicting goals. Alec wants to evade taxes without being caught. If he evades and the government does not audit, he wins by keeping the money he should have paid in taxes. If the government audits, the best action by Alec is to comply to avoid fines. The government, on the other hand, wants to catch tax evaders. It benefits from auditing tax evaders by fining them. The government also benefits from collecting the full amount of taxes owed. However, if Alec is already complying, it is costly to monitor the tax records just to find nothing.

The outcome of the game depends on how the taxpayer's decision to evade or comply interacts with the government's decision to audit or not audit. If the taxpayer evades and the government audits, Alec will face a fine and be forced to pay the taxes. But if the government does not audit, Alec keeps the money they owe. Conversely, if Alec complies and the government audits, Alec has nothing to fear but the government wastes resources on an unnecessary audit.

		Government	
		Audit	Not Audit
Alec	Comply	$(-T,T-C)$	$(-T,T)$
	Evade	$(-F,F-C)$	$(0,0)$

If Alec evades and the government audits, Alec pays a fine, F, a number larger than the tax amount, while the government gets F and pays the cost of auditing, C. This is a loss for Alec but a gain for the government. If Alec evades and the government does not audit, then Alec does not pay anything, and the government does not get any revenue.

If Alec complies, he pays T and the government collects T. If the government audits, it incurs cost C, resulting in a net payoff of $T-C$. If the government does not audit and Alec complies, it does not incur any cost and just receives the tax revenue T.

Just like in Matching Pennies, both players are engaged in a strategic interaction where their actions depend on predicting what the other player will do. However, unlike in Matching Pennies, this tax evasion game is not necessarily a zero-sum game. In some of the outcomes, the total payoffs can be negative due to the audit costs.

Now, let's calculate the Nash equilibrium of this game. Alec's decision to evade or comply depends on the probability that the government audits. Let's denote this probability with "g". If the government audits, evading leads to a payoff of $-F$, while the payoff for complying is $-T$. If the government does not audit, evading yields 0, while complying yields $-T$.

Alec will evade if the expected payoff of evading is greater than the payoff of complying, which is always $-T$. This occurs when

$$g * (-F) + (1 - g) * 0 > -T.$$

Rearranging terms show that Alec evades when

$$g < \frac{T}{F}.$$

Note that as the fine F is bigger than T, the ratio T/F is a number less than 1. So, if the probability of audit, g, is close enough to 1, Alec prefers to comply, but if g is low enough, he prefers to evade.

The government's decision to audit or not audit depends on the expected payoff from auditing, which depends on Alec's probability of evading. Let's denote this probability with "e". If Alec evades, auditing yields $F - C$, while not auditing gives 0. If Alec complies, auditing yields $T - C$, while not auditing gives T.

The government will audit if the expected payoff of auditing is greater than the expected payoff of not auditing. This occurs when

$$e(F) + (1 - e)T - C > (1 - e)T.$$

Simplifying,

$$e > \frac{C}{F}.$$

This inequality suggests that the government will audit if the probability of tax evasion is high enough to cover the audit cost.

At the mixed equilibrium, both players must be indifferent between their corresponding two strategies. This happens when both probabilities, g and e, are equal to the thresholds we calculated above. That is,

$$g = \frac{T}{F} \quad \text{and} \quad e = \frac{C}{F}.$$

If the amount of tax, T, increases, the probability of auditing rises, while if the fine, F, increases both probabilities of evasion and audit decrease. This might seem counterintuitive at first because when F is higher, the government has more to gain from auditing. However, for a correct interpretation, we need to remember that these probabilities are designed to keep both parties indifferent between their two strategies.

For instance, the equilibrium probability g keeps Alec indifferent between evading and complying. If the fine F is higher, Alec stands to lose more from evasion. This is reflected in the negative relation between the probability e and F. As a result, the government must decrease the probability of auditing to maintain Alec's indifference.

Let's think a bit more about the implication of tax levels on the probability of evasion. According to the simple model we have, when comparing two firms with different revenue streams, we would find that smaller firms, with lower tax levels required to be paid, are less likely to be monitored, while larger firms are more likely. Relatedly, the fine the firms must pay in case they evade taxes and get caught could also increase with the firms' size. However, the cost of auditing these small firms may still be relatively high. This would imply that smaller firms with smaller fines but relatively higher costs of auditing would be more likely to evade taxes, according to our simple model.

It is possible to confirm this prediction from our daily interactions. For instance, small shops sometimes offer their customers a discount if they agree to pay in cash. If the customer agrees, the shop owner can hide the transaction from tax authorities. This type of behaviour is especially common in developing countries, where street vendors or small restaurants often require payment in cash to avoid taxes.

In contrast, larger firms and corporations typically record all their transactions. Think about a large supermarket chain: when was the last time a cashier offered you a discount if you paid in cash and didn't ask for a receipt?

Another implication of our game is that when the cost of auditing decreases, the probability of tax evasion also goes down. This is intuitive because, with lower auditing costs, it becomes easier for the government to conduct audits.

As a result, to keep the government indifferent between auditing and not auditing, Alec reduces the probability of evasion.

What factors can reduce the cost of auditing? One of the key factors is the fiscal capacity of the state, a crucial concept in the field of Political Economy. Fiscal capacity refers to the ability of a state or government to raise revenue through taxation and other means to fund public goods, services, and overall governance. A state's fiscal capacity is higher when, among other things, it has an efficient and transparent administrative system for managing tax records, processing payments, and monitoring economic activities.

In their paper, "Why do developing countries tax so little?" Timothy Besley and Torsten Persson empirically document that the ratio of tax revenues to a country's aggregate income decreases as the country's income level rises. In other words, developing countries with lower gross domestic product (GDP) tend to have proportionately lower tax revenues than more developed countries. Our simple game above suggests that one possible explanation for this pattern is that developing countries have lower levels of fiscal capacity, making it harder for their governments to effectively audit firms.

Lower fiscal capacity can create a vicious cycle. When a state has low fiscal capacity, even a well-intentioned government may struggle to collect enough tax revenue to make the necessary investments in administrative infra-structure. Lower tax revenues lead to lower fiscal capacity, and lower fiscal capacity leads to lower tax revenues. As a result, developing countries often find themselves trapped in a low-income and low-tax equilibrium, where breaking the cycle is extremely difficult.

******

In the games of Matching Pennies and tax evasion, we saw how controlling the expectations of players might be strategically important. In these games, both players prefer to be unpredictable and use probabilistic strategies to do that. We later on explore this idea a bit further with the games of incomplete information.

Chapter 10

The Ultimatum Game: Mr. Charles' Will

It matters a lot for a game theoretical analysis if the game is a static game or dynamic one. For instance, consider the difference between the rock-paper-scissors (where you both pick your moves at the same time) and a chess match, where each player takes turns as they observe each other's moves. In static games, decision-makers move either simultaneously or without knowing what the others have chosen. The games we have discussed so far are all static games. Take "sealed-bid second-price auction" from earlier. In that example, bidders submit their orders in sealed envelopes without a chance of peeking into each other's bid. Then, it does not matter who submits their bid first because once the bids are revealed, no one gets a do-over. In contrast, players interacting in a dynamic setting either observe each other's moves, as in a chess game, or at least receive some information related to that.

Dynamic Game: A game that involves sequential moves by different players, such as repeated games or games with sequential moves.

Ultimatum Game: A two-stage extensive form game where one player can make a single offer to split a given sum, and the other player can either accept or reject the offer. If rejected, both players receive nothing.

Unlike in simultaneous-move or static games, bargaining situations often unfold like in the Ultimatum Game. In this game, the bargaining has a dynamic nature. The rules are simple: one player makes an offer, and the other player gets to look at it and decide whether to accept or reject. If they accept, the proposed allocation of whatever they are splitting goes through. If they reject, no one gets a penny.

To bring the Ultimatum Game to life, the next story gives you a perfect example of how real people's behaviour in this game can sometimes go against what you might expect from standard game theory. In fact, it's a great reminder that behavioural economics often paints a different picture from what the most common assumptions used in game theory might predict.

10.1. How to Issue an Ultimatum?

Mr. Charles had been living a quiet, single life for the past ten years. A wealthy man nearing his 80s, he figured it was high time to get his will in order. Easy, right? Well, not exactly. His beloved wife, Mrs. Victoria, had passed away a decade earlier after a tough battle with cancer, and their two sons, William and Edward, had never been the best of friends. In fact, their relationship, always a bit rocky, hit an all-time low right after their mother's funeral.

Edward lived abroad and visited his father in London once a year. During these visits, he made it very clear he didn't want to see William – or William's family. On the rare occasion, Mr. Charles invited both sons to dinner without giving Edward the heads-up, the brothers would start arguing at the table, and soon enough, both would storm out, leaving Mr. Charles sitting alone with an awkward silence and a half-finished roast.

With his wife gone and no family dinners to look forward to, Mr. Charles threw himself into his passion: supporting the arts. With his growing frustration with his sons, he even considered the idea of leaving everything to charity just to punish them. After listening to his friends telling him repeatedly that this would be extreme, he decided to give his sons a chance.

If William and Edward could somehow agree on how to split the inheritance, they would get to share it. If not, it is all going to charity! Of course, Mr. Charles knew the chances of these two agreeing on anything were about as likely as a peaceful family dinner, so he had to lay out the rules of the game very clearly. If he did not, they would end up in destructive heated arguments over the inheritance.

To give his sons a fighting chance to reach an agreement, Mr. Charles thought it would be best if they didn't have to meet face-to-face. That would just end in disaster. Instead, everything would go through a solicitor and a lawyer. Since Edward was doing financially better than William, Mr. Charles decided to kick things off in a way that would seem to favour William. William would make an offer to Edward on how to divide the estate. If Edward accepted, they'd split it accordingly. But if he rejected the offer, the whole estate would go to charity.

Mr. Charles couldn't help but imagine how this might unfold. Even if William offered Edward just 1% of the inheritance, technically, it would be better for Edward to accept than to walk away with nothing. "If a robot made the offer, Edward would definitely take it," Mr. Charles mused. "But since it's William, he might turn down anything that isn't a 50–50 split." Feeling a bit unsure, Mr. Charles decided to call up his nephew, Henry, who had studied Game Theory at university, for a little expert advice.

When they met, Henry sat his uncle down and carefully laid it all out for him. "Uncle Charles," Henry began, "what you've described is a classic example of the Ultimatum Game in Game Theory. In situations like these, where everyone knows the rules of the game (common knowledge) and can see what everyone else stands to gain (complete information), there's something we call the subgame perfect Nash equilibrium.

"Basically, in these perfect information games, where players take turns and can see each other's moves, we use a method called 'Backward Induction' to figure out the best possible decisions. It's intuitive, actually. We start from the last stage of the game and work our way back to the first. At each step, we cross off the bad decisions and keep only the best responses. By the time we get to the beginning, we're left with the Subgame Perfect Nash Equilibrium. In most games like this, there's only one right way to go about it."

Complete Information Game: A game in game theory where players have immediate and complete knowledge of each other's payoffs and actions.

Subgame: A part of an extensive form game that starts from a particular history and includes all subsequent actions, players making decisions, and resulting outcomes and histories. This subgame is embedded within the larger extensive form game.

Subgame Perfect Equilibrium: A strategy list in an extensive form game where the strategy constitutes a Nash equilibrium in every subgame of the game. The key difference between this concept and the Nash equilibrium is that it requires players to make the best possible response in all possible scenarios.

Backward Induction: A method used in finite extensive form games to determine the equilibrium strategies by starting at the last decision node and working backwards, marking the most profitable moves or Nash equilibria in subgames with simultaneous moves.

"So," Mr. Charles asked, leaning in with curiosity, "What kind of outcome should we expect in this situation?" Henry replied, "Well, Uncle Charles, Edward's going to get the short end of the stick here. William will end up with nearly everything. Why? Because even if William offers Edward only a tiny slice of the estate, it's still better than nothing. Knowing that, William could offer Edward 1% or even 0.1%, and Edward will grudgingly accept it."

Mr. Charles frowned. "But what about Edward's pride? Would he really accept such a lopsided deal?"

Henry thought for a moment, then shrugged. "Pride could definitely play a role here. But this is a topic from Behavioural Economics," he replied.

He scratched his head and then added, "Actually, we could get a second opinion. My old university friend Ruth studied Behavioural Economics after we graduated. She is much smarter than me in this area. I hope she still remembers me."

A few days later, they all met for tea at a charming café. Ruth, with her big smile, warmly greeted Henry and Mr. Charles. "Henry! It's been ages! What have you been up to?"

After the usual catching-up chatter, Mr. Charles explained the inheritance situation. "So, Ruth, in real life, does this Ultimatum Game, as Henry calls it, usually end with the proposer – William in this case – getting almost the whole pie?"

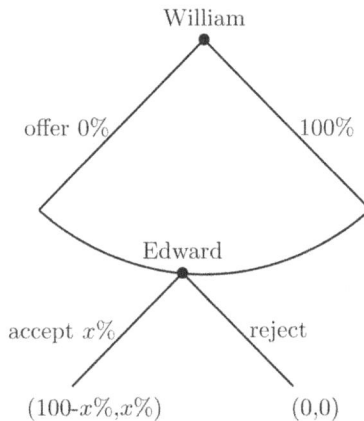

William

offer 0%   100%

Edward

accept x%   reject

$(100-x\%,x\%)$ $(0,0)$

Ruth chuckled. "If people only cared about cold, hard cash, then yes, William would take most of it. But," she said, "there's a bit more to people than just greed. Social and cultural factors come into play." She paused, letting that sink in. "It can even depend on the ages of the players. It is different, if you had two little kids or you have two adults.

Ruth continued, "First of all, backward induction works great when everyone knows all the material and emotional stakes in the game. But here, William might know how much money Edward would gain, but he doesn't know what kind of emotional cost his brother might be willing to endure. And that changes things. All those lab experiments we've done with adults show that people often reject super low offers, even if it means walking away empty-handed, just to make a point. And proposers know this too, so they tend to offer at least 40% of the pie on average. Sometimes, just to avoid a rejection, they'll go for a straight 50–50 split – which is almost always accepted."

Ruth leaned back and smiled. "So, Mr. Charles, don't be too surprised if your sons end up being a little more generous with each other than what Henry expects."

Mr. Charles was all smiles after hearing Ruth's explanation, feeling a bit more hopeful that his sons might actually cooperate for once. He thanked Henry and Ruth warmly and, in a moment of inspiration, asked Ruth if she'd be willing to serve as a consultant after the will was read. "You know," he said, "just in case things get a bit … tense." Ruth, always one to embrace the unexpected, happily agreed, especially when Mr. Charles mentioned a rather generous fee for her services. "Looks like all that time studying Game Theory will finally pay off," she laughed.

With renewed energy, Mr. Charles went home, sat down at his desk, and began drafting his will. He was ready to give his sons one last chance at working things out. Working with his solicitor, he crafted the following conditions:

Clause 1: After Mr. Charles' departure, the solicitor would promptly send a letter to both William and Edward, explaining the process for dividing the estate. This letter would, naturally, be delivered with a suitable amount of legal drama.

Clause 2: William and Edward were each required to meet separately with Ruth. If either of them refused, the entire estate would go to the other brother. And if they both refused, it would go to the charities.

Clause 3: Once the meetings with Ruth were completed, William would submit his offer for the division of the estate to the solicitor and notary, who would then pass the offer along to Edward. All very official, with plenty of time for each brother to stew in their thoughts.

Clause 4: If Edward accepted William's offer, they would both receive their shares, just as William proposed. However, if Edward decided to reject the offer, the entire estate would again go to charity.

Five years after Mr. Charles penned his cleverly crafted will, he passed away, leaving William and Edward to face the terms of the Ultimatum Game their father had set up for them. Both brothers met with Ruth to hear her advice. William, who now had the unenviable task of making an offer, proposed giving Edward 45% of the estate, worth around £900,000 at the time. It wasn't half, but it was close enough – at least in William's mind.

When Edward received the offer, he was livid. "How dare he offer me only 45%?" he fumed. "I am already doing well, I can reject it just to teach him a lesson!" This, of course, was exactly what William had feared. Despite his wife Emma's gentle advice of "Don't be greedy, just offer him half," William had dug in his heels. "Let's see if Edward has the guts to turn this down," he had said. But he was stressed out about the outcome.

On the other side of town, Edward was pacing up and down, muttering about his "scoundrel of a brother." He was moments away from rejecting the offer out of sheer pride when his wife, Grace, stepped in with a calm, practical reminder: "£900,000 isn't exactly pocket change, Edward. Think about it – if the tables were turned, what would you have offered William?" Edward stopped in his tracks, thought it over, and with a rueful smile admitted, "You're right. Honestly, I probably wouldn't have offered him more than £800,000. And if it was not for the stuff that I learned from Ruth, I would have offered him £10, just for the fun of it."

With that bit of reflection – and Grace's gentle nudge – Edward reluctantly told the solicitor and notary that he would accept William's offer.

Meanwhile, when the news reached William, he let out a massive sigh of relief, as if the weight of the world had finally been lifted off his shoulders. That evening, he celebrated with his family at home, raising his glass of whiskey to his father's portrait hanging on the wall. By the third glass, William's eyes grew misty, and he stared at the portrait with a mix of emotions.

Over at Edward's house, a similar scene played out. There were smiles, laughter, and perhaps a few tears as Edward realized that, despite his initial anger, things had not turned out too badly. Whether the brothers ever fully reconciled remained a mystery, but Emma and Grace were spending a lot of afternoons shopping together on Oxford Street.

Chapter 11

Room for Negotiation: Credible Threats and Backward Induction

Four years ago, when Tom and Sarah got married, they rented their cosy little apartment, a perfect spot nestled conveniently between their workplaces. Two years later, they welcomed a child into their life. They loved the neighbourhood; it was safe and had good schools for their child. With their income level, it would be too much of a stretch to purchase an apartment so they preferred to settle in this for a longer term.

Their landlady, Mrs. Walker, had always been pretty pleased with them too. Tom and Sarah were the model tenants – always on time with rent, taking care of the property like it was their own. Over the years, they'd come to a mutual understanding about the rent increases. Until this year, the rent has increased with relatively small increments around the official inflation rate. The current rent is £1,000 a month, a bit underpriced compared to the market price. However, for Mrs. Walker, the rent was fine as it helped pay off the last bits of her mortgage and kept her bills covered, with her pension filling in the gaps.

But two years ago, things took a sharp turn when inflation went through the roof, and suddenly, Mrs. Walker's pension and rental income were not enough to support her lifestyle. The bills and the petrol prices became so high that short summer trips to Spain were becoming a luxury that she could not afford anymore. So, there had to be a rent hike for her to keep her purchasing power.

Meanwhile, Tom and Sarah were also feeling the heat from the inflation. In addition to the increases in the daily expenses, the current day-care prices were increasing as well. As they are expecting similar increases in the future education costs, they were trying to increase savings earmarked for education. Furthermore, there were rumours of a coming wave of layouts at their jobs. In light of these, a rent increase was intolerable. They decided to ask Mrs. Walker to keep the rent at its current level.

When it was time to renew the lease, Mrs. Walker decided to ask for a whopping £2,000 a month. She thought that this was only fair as the market rate of similar apartments was a bit lower. She figured Tom and Sarah wouldn't want to leave just to save a few hundred pounds – they'd worked so hard to build a life in the house. Sure, they might grumble, but in the end, they'd pay up rather than deal with the hassle of moving.

Mrs. Walker visited Sarah and Tom at their home. When the three sat down to discuss the rent, Mrs. Walker started with a tone that was somewhere between stern and sympathetic. She began explaining how the economic crisis had hit her hard, how prices everywhere had gone up, and how rents in the neighbourhood were climbing. Then, she hit them with the big one: "I'm proposing a new rent of £2,000 per month."

Tom and Sarah were absolutely shocked. Two grand? How could Mrs. Walker make such an offer? She had been such a nice landlady so far. She always agreed to incremental increases in the rent. Surely, it was not impossible for them to gather the budget for an additional £1,000. But that would mean a lot of sacrifice and possibly less funds towards the education savings. Besides, Sarah reasoned, Mrs. Walker needed them to stay. It is hard for her to find a new tenant as reliable as they are. Sarah quickly recovered from the shock and launched into an explanation of their own struggles. The same crisis had pinched their wallets too, and with increasing pressures for education savings, she firmly told Mrs. Walker that a rent increase was impossible. In fact, they were hoping for no increase at all.

Now, it was Mrs. Walker's turn to be shocked. After taking a moment to collect herself, she responded with a threat. "I won't agree to any lower increase and if you don't, I'll have to ask you to leave and I'll take you to court if I have to!" With that, she turned on her heel and left, leaving Tom and Sarah sitting in their living room, still trying to process what had just happened.

Mrs. Walker returned home feeling more perplexed than victorious. Why on earth were Tom and Sarah being so stubborn? She had expected a little resistance, sure, but not this total rejection of the rent increase. Given their jobs and the hassle of moving, it seemed like agreeing to the higher rent should have been fine. Were they just digging in their heels to spite her?

She toyed with the idea of sending a formal notice to start the legal process in case they reject the increase. But as she thought more about this, a lower rent increase started to seem more appealing than this bitter end with her reliable tenants. It would be too much hassle with the legal process of forcing her tenants to leave the apartment, and finding new tenants. Afterall, given the current prices and the market rates she would be fine with £1,500.

Meanwhile, back at Tom and Sarah's place, they were also starting to feel the weight of their defiance. At first, they had felt confident in standing their ground, but Mrs. Walker's threat left them confused a bit. Sarah started to remember their chats with Mrs. Walker. She realized that with the recent inflation, it could have become harder to live with her pension and the rent.

However, £2,000 was just too much. This was a bit over the market price. Furthermore, she would have accepted a price that is even a bit lower than the market price instead of spending many months with low or no rent while kicking them out and trying to find new tenants. Sarah made a quick calculation and decided that £1,500 was more than enough. Mrs. Walker made a non-credible threat by asking for £2,000 but she should agree to £1,500.

> **Non-Credible Threat:** A situation in an extensive form game where a player's strategy does not include the best response in a future scenario. Such a strategy is not credible to other players because they expect the player to deviate from it in certain scenarios.
>
> **Credible Threat:** A situation in an extensive form game where a player's strategy includes the best response in all future scenarios.

A few days later, Mrs. Walker reached out to Tom and Sarah, suggesting they meet again. Sarah immediately realized that this was a sign of compromise. Mrs. Walker should have realized that her offer was not reasonable. When they arrived at her house, there was a noticeable difference in the air – less tension, more "let's get this sorted." Mrs. Walker, now aware that a 100% increase was off the table, offered her compromise of £1,500.

Tom and Sarah exchanged a look. Sarah was right in her calculations. The days of incremental increases were behind them, and they realized they wouldn't come out on top if they pushed their luck any further. So, with a shared nod and a sigh of relief, they agreed to Mrs. Walker's 50% increase.

When Mrs. Walker first proposed that 100% rent increase, she had all the confidence that the tenants would accept it. But after seeing their shocked faces and hearing Sarah's firm refusal, Mrs. Walker began to realize that she had overplayed her hand. Tom and Sarah weren't just being stubborn when they rejected her first proposal. They knew she wasn't going to risk a costly and time-consuming transition. As she sat there, sipping her tea and reflecting on how things played out, she regretted the drama her 100% demand had caused. "Why did I even go there?" she thought.

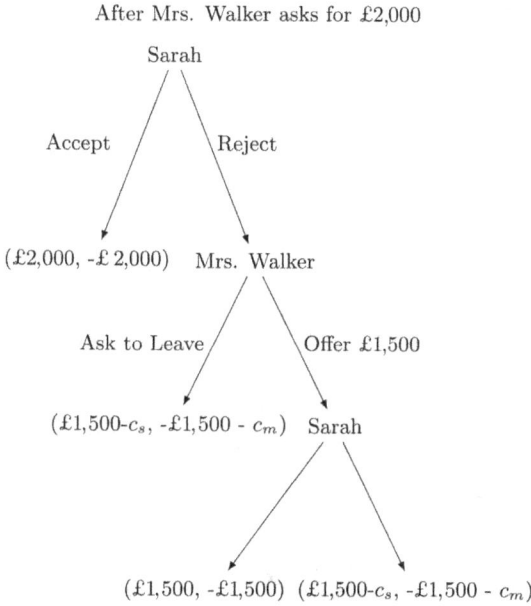

After Mrs. Walker asks for £2,000

Sarah

Accept / \ Reject

(£2,000, -£2,000)   Mrs. Walker

Ask to Leave / \ Offer £1,500

$(£1,500-c_s, -£1,500 - c_m)$ Sarah

$(£1,500, -£1,500)$ $(£1,500-c_s, -£1,500 - c_m)$

In game theory, Mrs. Walker's initial threat to reject any increase lower than 100% was what's called a non-credible threat. It sounds intimidating, but when you look closely, it doesn't hold up. Tom and Sarah, being smart tenants, realized that Mrs. Walker could actually settle to a lower increase.

The game tree above illustrates the events that take place after Mrs. Walker's initial offer of £2,000. Mrs. Walker threatened Sarah and Tom by asking them to leave if Sarah rejects £2,000. If Sarah believed this threat and rejected this offer, she would expect to move out. In this case, suppose that they would expect to find a new apartment at the market price, which is £1,500. However, moving out is costly, and let that cost be some positive number $c_m > 0$. Sarah and Tom may very well want to avoid this outcome and accept this offer. However, this threat was not credible, so Sarah did not believe that Mrs. Walker would actually ask them to leave. To see this, let's apply backward induction. If Mrs. Walker makes another offer at £1,500 after the initial rejection of Sarah, Sarah would definitely accept this offer instead of moving out. Now, Mrs. Walker understands that if she offers £1,500, Sarah would accept it. Then, if she asks them to leave, she has to search for new tenants. This search process could be costly, and let that cost be some positive number $c_s > 0$. At this stage, the best option for Mrs. Walker is to offer £1,500 and not worry about searching for new tenants. Therefore, Sarah can figure out that Mrs. Walker's threat is credible as once Sarah rejects the initial offer, she understands that it is in the best interest of Mrs. Walker to make a concession of £1,500.

This concept of non-credible threats is a staple in dynamic games. For a threat to be credible, when it comes to carrying it out, the action corresponding to the threat has to be the best option for the person making it. If not, other players can infer that the threatening player would not go through with it and so just ignore the threat altogether.

In dynamic games, non-credible threats are swiftly eliminated when calculating Subgame Perfect Nash Equilibrium (SPNE), which works a bit differently from the standard Nash equilibrium that suits more to static games. When it comes to games where everyone can see each other's moves and the payoffs of the other players, SPNE can be calculated by using backward induction. In backward induction, every move in the game must be the best response in every possible scenario, and so strategies involving non-credible threats are eliminated.

Backward induction enables the first players to correctly predict the future plays and form their expectations accordingly. We can apply this method to the rent negotiation example between Mrs. Walker and Sarah.

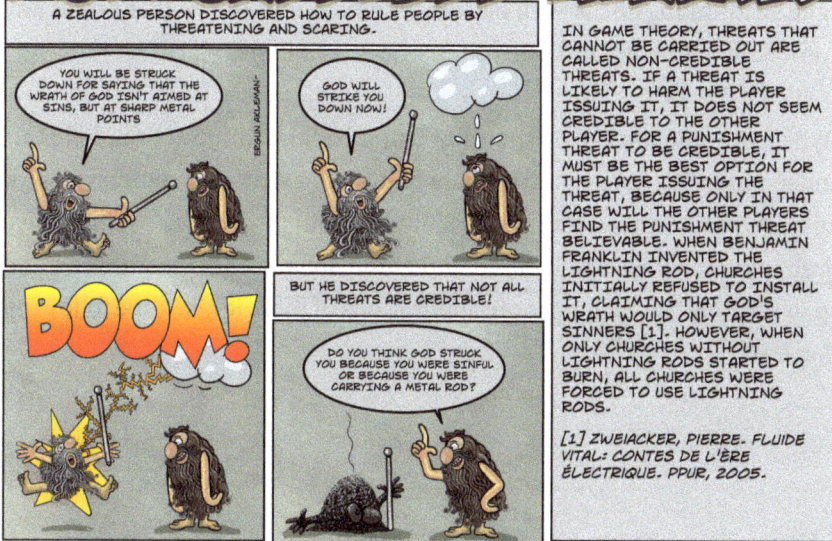

NON-CREDIBLE THREATS

A ZEALOUS PERSON DISCOVERED HOW TO RULE PEOPLE BY THREATENING AND SCARING.

YOU WILL BE STRUCK DOWN FOR SAYING THAT THE WRATH OF GOD ISN'T AIMED AT SINS, BUT AT SHARP METAL POINTS

GOD WILL STRIKE YOU DOWN NOW!

BOOM!

BUT HE DISCOVERED THAT NOT ALL THREATS ARE CREDIBLE!

DO YOU THINK GOD STRUCK YOU BECAUSE YOU WERE SINFUL OR BECAUSE YOU WERE CARRYING A METAL ROD?

IN GAME THEORY, THREATS THAT CANNOT BE CARRIED OUT ARE CALLED NON-CREDIBLE THREATS. IF A THREAT IS LIKELY TO HARM THE PLAYER ISSUING IT, IT DOES NOT SEEM CREDIBLE TO THE OTHER PLAYER. FOR A PUNISHMENT THREAT TO BE CREDIBLE, IT MUST BE THE BEST OPTION FOR THE PLAYER ISSUING THE THREAT, BECAUSE ONLY IN THAT CASE WILL THE OTHER PLAYERS FIND THE PUNISHMENT THREAT BELIEVABLE. WHEN BENJAMIN FRANKLIN INVENTED THE LIGHTNING ROD, CHURCHES INITIALLY REFUSED TO INSTALL IT, CLAIMING THAT GOD'S WRATH WOULD ONLY TARGET SINNERS [1]. HOWEVER, WHEN ONLY CHURCHES WITHOUT LIGHTNING RODS STARTED TO BURN, ALL CHURCHES WERE FORCED TO USE LIGHTNING RODS.

[1] ZWEIACKER, PIERRE. FLUIDE VITAL: CONTES DE L'ÈRE ÉLECTRIQUE. PPUR, 2005.

Let's start at the end: if Tom and Sarah refuse any proposed rent increase, Mrs. Walker has two choices – either start with the legal process and start looking for a new tenant or come up with a more reasonable increase that Tom and Sarah would accept. If she insists on a 100% increase, she knows that there will be some legal period for Tom and Sarah to find a new apartment and move. Furthermore, there are some uncertainties about the market. What if the new tenants are not as reliable as Tom and Sarah? This makes her threat of not accepting anything lower than non-credible. However, with a 50% increase, Mrs. Walker would avoid the hassle and could immediately start receiving a higher rent.

Knowing this, Tom and Sarah can safely reject the 100% increase because they understand Mrs. Walker wouldn't go through with it. But if she proposes a 50% increase, and they reject it, looking for a new tenant at the market price would start looking like a more appealing option to Mrs. Walker.

With this knowledge, Mrs. Walker's best move is clear: propose a 50% increase – the highest amount Tom and Sarah would accept without a fight. By thinking ahead with backward induction, Mrs. Walker avoids any non-credible threats, and everyone's strategies fall into place.

Dynamic game analysis, especially using backward induction, helps us understand situations like corporate battles, international standoffs, or, in this case, rent disputes. It shows how even seemingly complex conflicts have clear solutions if we think ahead and eliminate any bluffs that don't stand up to scrutiny. We explore more applications of these ideas in the following chapters!

Chapter 12

The Self-Defence of Monopoly: Entry Deterrence and Commitment Strategies

James was ready to pop open a bottle of champagne to celebrate the grand opening of his second café in his small town. The university students have been keeping his first place quite busy. Looking at the long queue in front of the register, he is sure that this second café will make good profits as well. He was already enjoying thoughts of opening a third place.

Then, the representative from the coffee bean company, Ms. Martin, has arrived. James ordered her favourite coffee. It was time to finalize the details of the agreement on coffee bean shipments for the second place.

Towards the end, he bragged about his success in the first café and added that he is expecting the same from the second branch. "Maybe" he added, "we will soon renew our agreement, when I open the third branch." Ms. Martin replied with a serious tone,

"Let me lend you a secret. There are some rumours that the Star Café chain is planning to expand to smaller towns." She concluded, "you might face some competition in near future."

Still sitting at the table after Ms. Martin left, James stared blankly at his laptop, the joy of opening his second branch completely evaporated. He had barely wrapped his head around running two locations, and now he was imagining Star Café's flashy storefront just a few doors down, offering loyalty points, free Wi-Fi, and lower prices for the most popular standard drinks.

James knew he had two options: play nice or go to war. The first option, the sensible one, meant adjusting to the new reality. He'd have to lower his prices, maybe add a few "buy one, get one free" deals, and accept that the days of making a fortune from extra shots of espresso were over. His two cafés would still survive, but they'd be running at a slower pace, and his dream of a third branch might have to wait. It wasn't glamorous, but it would pay the bills.

Then, there was the second option: wage an all-out price war. He could drop his prices so low that Star Café would think twice about setting up camp in his city. Of course, this approach would be risky. He might take down Star Café for a while, but it would probably drain his bank account. By the time the dust settled, James could be out of business, left with nothing but memories of his once-thriving cafés.

Ms. Martin had kept a few key details to herself during her conversation with James. At that London meeting, one topic of hot debate was how local café owners might react to Star Café's entry into their markets. Would they fight back with aggressive price cuts, or would they simply roll over and adapt to the new reality? Star Café's team figured that if local cafés tried to wage a full-blown price war, it might not be worth expanding into those markets at all. But if the locals accepted the inevitable and adjusted, Star Café could happily expand.

But, of course, figuring out how the local café owners would react wasn't as simple as pulling a rabbit out of a hat. They needed data – specifically, details about the local cafés' income and sales. That's why Star Café had invited Ms. Martin to the meeting in the first place. As the supplier for both James's café and Star Café, Ms. Martin had a bird's-eye view of the situation. Plus, it was in her company's best interest for everyone to stay in business – more cafés, more coffee beans sold, more profits all around. It was a win-win for her team, no matter who dominated the local scene.

During the meeting, Ms. Martin hadn't held back when it came to dishing out advice. Based on the sales data she had, she'd told Star Café that local cafés like James's wouldn't survive long if they tried to slash prices to compete with a giant like Star Café. It was a doomed strategy, and eventually, the local guys would be forced to either adapt or close up shop for good. Star Café's team loved hearing this – it made their decision much easier.

And that's where backward induction comes into play. With Ms. Martin's insights, Star Café knew exactly what to expect. If they opened new branches in cities like James's, local cafés wouldn't be able to afford a price war and would eventually adapt to the new competition.

Meanwhile, back in his café, James had no idea that the decision to enter his market had already been made in a meeting room far away. As he sipped his espresso and pondered his next move, little did he know he was already part of a game where the major players had figured out how the story would end long before he even knew he was in it.

For James, adapting to the competition and accepting lower profit margins was the only real way forward. But James had never been in the café game purely for the money. His first café had been a passion project, a way to prove to himself that he could succeed. He'd taken pride in being hands-on, overseeing every little detail, from the coffee beans to the comfy chairs, and his second branch was the result of that hard-earned success. Competing with a giant like Star Café was daunting, sure, but it also offered him a new challenge: to stand his ground and build his brand. In a way, this was another chance for James to prove he could hold his own, even against the big players.

Meanwhile, in a neighbouring city, things were quite different for another café owner, David. Like James, David had opened his first café on the busiest street two years ago, but David's city was larger, and so were his ambitions. He had started with more capital and, from day one, had his sights set on rapid expansion. While James had taken a personal approach, David had no interest in being behind the counter or fussing over coffee machines. His goal was to grow fast and dominate the market.

David's bold strategy hadn't come out of thin air – it had been cooked up by his old university friend, Rachel. Back in their student days, Rachel had always been the one with the sharpest business instincts. She had big dreams of becoming a CEO of a large corporation and knew that building a fast-growing café chain like David's could be the perfect springboard to catch the eye of major corporations. When David shared his idea of opening a café, Rachel immediately saw the potential and laid out a grand vision for him – one that involved rapid expansion and, of course, lots of profits.

But Rachel had also warned David about a lurking threat: big chains like Star Café. She knew they could one day enter his market, posing a serious challenge to his empire-building plans. If David didn't grow fast enough, he could find himself out of business before he even had a chance to make a name for himself. Her solution was to expand aggressively, build a strong presence, and be ready to slash prices if Star Café ever tried to muscle in. That way, they'd be forced to think twice before entering his territory.

Rachel was confident in her plan and had even more confidence in her ability to execute it. She suggested that David hand over the reins of the business to her for a few years, assuring him that her leadership would ensure the company's rapid growth. She suggested adding a clause to their contract that ties the hands of David on managerial decisions. For David, this seemed like a win-win situation. He'd get to focus on the big picture without having to worry about the day-to-day grind, and Rachel would drive the business forward. According to the contract, David would delegate all managerial decisions for three years, as long as Rachel didn't make losses. All profits would be reinvested into expanding the café chain as fast as possible, and if Rachel hit her ambitious growth targets, she'd become a partner in the business.

> **Strategic Delegation:** In game theory, strategic delegation is when a player delegates future decision-making power to another player to prevent short-term gains from undermining long-term profits. This solves the commitment problem by binding the player to a strategy.

Ms. Martin, who had previously worked with Rachel on coffee bean contracts, had seen her management style in action. When the folks at Star Café discussed expanding into David's city at their London meeting, Ms. Martin offered a bit of inside knowledge. "The local café chain you're talking about is managed by someone who will stop at nothing to grow that business," she said. "Rachel's not just going to roll over and watch Star Café take her market share. If it comes down to it, she'll drop prices so low, it'll hurt Star Café's bottom line."

"But wait," one of the Star Café representatives chimed in, "wouldn't the café owner, David, step in if things got too crazy and profits started vanishing?" Ms. Martin smiled knowingly. "Not quite. David has given Rachel full control over the café chain, and according to their contract, he can't interfere for three years. She's running the show."

This revelation put a wrinkle in Star Café's expansion plans. After looking into it further, they realized that entering David's city would mean making a loss. It was just not worth the hassle from a mid-sized city, while there are many other options of expansion.

This scenario, as outlined, is a classic example of a market entry game in game theory. The typical expectation in these situations is that big chains like Star Café enter new markets, and local businesses adapt to survive. No one wants to risk bankruptcy by engaging in a price war they can't win. However, when a local café owner like David signs a contract that commits the manager to an aggressive strategy – like Rachel's aggressive approach – this changes the game. Now, there's a Nash equilibrium where Star Café decides to stay out of the market entirely, knowing they'd face a battle that could do more harm than good.

In the following chapter, we dive into the repeated Prisoner's Dilemma. Repeated games bring in new factors, like the discount rate, that change how players think about cooperation, competition, and long-term outcomes.

Chapter 13

Repeated Games: Can OPEC Countries Adhere to Their Quotas in the Long Run?

Let's revisit the OPEC example we had before, but this time, instead of treating it as a one-stage game, let's explore what happens when Iran and Venezuela face these choices year after year – a repeated game.

Previously, we saw that if both countries stick to their 1 million-barrel quotas, each makes $40 million annually. But if one cheats and pumps out 2 million barrels while the other sticks to the quota, the cheater walks away with $50 million, while the rule-follower is left with just $25 million. And if both decide to cheat by pumping out 2 million barrels, they each walk away with $30 million – a classic "Prisoner's Dilemma," where the temptation to defect leads to a mutually worse outcome.

Now, let's assume this isn't a one-shot deal but something Iran and Venezuela must decide every year. Modelling such an interaction as a repeated game will make our discussion more realistic. As we already introduced Backward Induction in the previous chapters, we can use it to analyze such a dynamic game.

> **Repeated games** are dynamic games in which the same game is played repeatedly, either for a finite or indefinite number of rounds. Each round in a repeated game is called a stage game.

A key distinction we make in the analysis of repeated games is about whether there is a certain deadline for the game – which is common knowledge among the players – or the deadline is uncertain. If the players all know when the game is going to end, there is a terminal stage of the game and we can apply backward induction from that stage backwards. If there is no certain deadline, but there is a probability that the game may continue from each stage on, the strategies have to take an indefinite future into account.

We can give a spoiler at this point. If Iran and Venezuela know when this agreement will end, at each stage where they play Prisoner's Dilemma, the outcome would be identical to the one-shot version, where they cannot cooperate and leave with worse payoffs. However, if they do not know when the game may end, they can choose their strategies as if they play the game infinitely many times. Then, a perfectly cooperative outcome becomes a possibility. Whether the countries follow such a cooperation depends on their patience, namely on their "discount factors". We elaborate on this term in the following.

Now, first suppose that Iran and Venezuela's oil ministers have a five-year run before they head off into retirement. During those five years, they agree to stick to their OPEC quotas. But each year, they're faced with the same tough decision – stick to the deal, or cheat by pumping extra oil. Neither minister knows at any stage whether the other minister is planning to cheat. They learn their opponent's move only in the following period.

Let's apply backward induction and start with the fifth and final year. By then, the oil ministers are thinking, "Well, there's no next year, so why not pump out a little extra oil? Who's going to care?" And since both ministers are thinking the same thing, they both increase the production to 2 million barrels each. As we know from the one-shot version of this game, this ends up with the worst outcome.

Now, we rewind to year four. The ministers know that in year five, they're both going to break the quota anyway, so what's the point of being nice now? They'll both break the quota in year four too. And guess what happens in year three, year two, and year one? The same thing – each year, they'll glance at their production levels and increase it, knowing full well the other guy will do the same.

Now, imagine the case where Iran and Venezuela do not know when the agreement will end. To make this scenario more concrete, suppose that the agreement is not done between the ministers with five-year terms but between institutions, each of which has an indefinite life ahead.

Each year, they both pledge to stick to their OPEC quotas, producing 1 million barrels and ensuring oil prices stay high. But there's a catch – the pledge comes with a condition: if one country cheats and cranks up production, the other country will unleash the full force of retaliation. And by retaliation, we mean both countries break their quotas for the rest of time, sending oil prices tumbling into the basement.

In this scenario, the best strategy for the country that first breaks the quota is to keep right on doing it, figuring, "Well, I've already made the first move, so might as well keep going." Meanwhile, the other country is forced to follow suit, and now everyone's stuck in an endless loop of overproduction and low prices. The agreement collapses like a sandcastle against the tide.

But here's the key question: Is that threat of retaliation even believable? In other words, would Venezuela really carry out its revenge if Iran cheats? Or is it all just talk? To answer this, we need to know one thing: how patient are these countries when it comes to money?

It all boils down to how they value today's money compared to tomorrow's. This is where the present value method comes in. Present value of a monetary value in a year is the answer to the following question: "How much money do I need right now to feel like I've made the same amount as I would a year from now?" To explain, let's say you're offered $1 million next year, but you'd rather get your hands on some cash now. With an interest rate of 100%, you'd only need $500,000 today to feel like a million bucks in a year – because that $500,000 would double in 12 months. In this case, the discount factor would be 0.5, as you would be discounting a million next year by half. But if the interest rate were a measly 1%, you'd need around $990,100 today to feel like you've got a million coming your way later. In this case, the discounting factor is approximately 0.9901.

> **Discount Factor:** The factor that determines how decision-makers value future returns compared to immediate returns. It reflects their preference for receiving the same amount of income now rather than later.

The higher the interest rate, the more impatient you are. High rates imply that you would prefer to have the cash now because you could invest it and watch it grow quickly. Low rates, on the other hand, mean you are fine with waiting, as your returns on immediate income would not be all that high. This "impatience" is what we call a low discount factor: countries with a low discount factor don't care as much about future profits because they can make better returns by focusing on the present.

So, if Venezuela is super impatient – meaning the interest rate is high – it will likely think, "I need my money now, forget about next year." And in that case, the threat of retaliation isn't so credible because who's going to sacrifice today's gains for the sake of a vague future punishment? But if both countries are more patient and the interest rates are low, they'll stick to the agreement longer, knowing that the steady income over time is better than blowing it all by cheating early.

In short, the more patient these countries are, the more likely they are to keep playing nice in the long game. Otherwise, it's a short-lived truce, followed by an all-out oil production frenzy.

In a world where everyone is relatively patient – let's say with a 0.9 as the discount factor, which corresponds to an approximate 11% interest rate – each country's oil ministers are essentially playing the long game. They're not just thinking about next year's paycheck, but about how their actions today will affect their bank accounts for years to come. If both countries stick to the OPEC quota of 1 million barrels, each will earn $40 million every year. The present value of earning $40 million per year, forever, is $400 million.

Now, let's imagine things start to get a little more tempting. One country – let's say Venezuela – decides to break the quota, thinking, "I can make $50 million this year while Iran plays by the rules." That's a nice bonus, but it's a one-time deal. After that, Iran, feeling thoroughly betrayed, will pump out 2 million barrels as well, and now both countries are stuck with just $30 million a year, forever. So, Venezuela's windfall comes at a long-term cost: instead of making $40 million annually, they'll be stuck with $30 million. Let's do some math here.

Using the discount factor fixed at 0.9, the present value of $40 million annually works out to a cool $40 million / (1 − 0.9) = $400 million. With that in mind, let's walk through the internal monologue of a country that's getting tempted by the idea of breaking its OPEC pledge:

"If I play by the rules and stick to the 1 million-barrel quota, my income's present value is a solid $400 million. But what if I, say, bend the rules a bit and pump out 2 million barrels? I would get $50 million this year. And after that, I would only be making $30 million a year. All those future $30 million payouts are worth 0.9 * ($30 million) / 0.1 = $270 million. So, breaking the pledge means I walk away with a total of $320 million. A decent haul, but definitely less than the $400 million I'd make by playing nice."

So, our would-be quota-breakers find themselves in a bit of a pickle. Sure, a quick $50 million sounds sweet, but when they run the numbers, they realize that sneaking a few extra barrels out today is not worth it.

In this high-patience scenario, no rational country would dream of breaking its pledge – it's like being offered a lifetime supply of chocolate and deciding to stick with it rather than grabbing just one bar. However, when patience is low and the annual interest rate spikes, things change. Suppose that the discount factor is 0.5, which corresponds to a 100% interest rate. With such a low discount factor, the present value of an annual income of $40 million drops to $80 million. You can almost hear the oil ministers thinking:

"If I behave myself and stick to the quota, sure, I get a steady flow of $40 million a year, but all that future money is worth way less to me now. In fact, it's only worth $80 million in total. But if I decide to live in the moment, break the quota, and go all-in with 2 million barrels, I can make $50 million right away. Plus, after that, I still get $30 million annually, and even those future payouts aren't looking so bad when I add them all up."

At this point, both countries see the quick $50 million payday as far more tempting than the slow and steady $40 million they'd earn from being well-behaved. So, in a low-patience scenario with a higher interest rate, everyone's grabbing what they can, when they can – because tomorrow feels a lot less valuable than today!

In this scenario, a country pondering whether to pump out 2 million barrels while the other sticks to the OPEC quota might think, "Well, if I play nice and follow the 1 million-barrel quota, I'll earn $40 million a year, forever. The present value of that income at today's rates is $80 million, so not bad. But, on the other hand, if I break the quota, I'll get $50 million right away, and after that, only $30 million a year for the rest of time. The present value of those future $30 million paydays comes out to $30 million. That gives me a grand total of $80 million. So, whether I play by the rules or break them, I'll end up with $80 million."

If the interest rate goes up even a little bit, the temptation to break the quota becomes too strong to resist. With a higher interest rate, the value of getting $50 million today outweighs the future losses, so both countries will be rushing to pump out those extra barrels. On the flip side, if the interest rate dips just a bit lower, suddenly patience is rewarded, and both countries will think, "Why bother cheating when we can rake in the steady cash forever?"

As we've explored, if Iran and Venezuela know when their little oil cartel agreement will expire, they'll fall back into the same trap as in the one-shot game. Greed will win, and they'll both pump out extra barrels, leaving everyone with lower profits. But if they do not know when the game will end, we get two very different possibilities. In a world where everyone's patient, the countries will stick to their OPEC quotas, sitting pretty and earning high profits for years to come. In a world where patience is in short supply, though, the temptation to cheat will prove irresistible, and they'll both crank out 2 million barrels, stuck with lower profits, just like in the one-shot game.

******

In the following chapter, we dive into a Political Economy game that uses the concept of subgame perfect Nash equilibrium, shining a spotlight on how patronage and staffing work behind the scenes in political systems.

Chapter 14

Patronage Cycles: Political Culture as a Subgame Perfect Equilibrium

Repeated interactions between two long-lived agents may have various outcomes depending on how cooperative the agents are. In many applications, there are subgame Nash equilibria with fully cooperative outcomes but also ones with no cooperation at all. As we discussed before with focal points, cultural factors play a crucial role in selecting one of the equilibria as the outcome of the game. This is because cultural factors enable agents to coordinate their expectations of each other's behaviour.

Electoral competition between two major political parties is a perfect example of a long-run repeated interaction. Consider an electoral regime with just two political parties: the Left and the Right. After each election, there is a winner and a loser. The winning party gets to form a government by appointing some of the party members to ministry positions. In many regimes, such an electoral victory is also accompanied by a legislative majority and the winning party gains some legislative power in addition to its executive.

How does a winning party use this political power? For instance, the winning party can push for legislation that would not be supported by the opposition party at all. Furthermore, they can fill all key bureaucratic positions with more loyalists. Such practices can be thought of as acquiring all of the public sources and throwing the opposition under the bus. This could look tempting for a winning party but of course the opposition can win the elections next time, and they can do the same.

Alternatively, the winning party can cooperate with the opposition to design bi-partisan legislation. They may leave some of the key positions to the opposition. That is, they can share the public sources with their rival. Such a cooperative behaviour can be sustainable only if it's reciprocated by their rival when they are in power. Otherwise, whatever trust is there between the parties might break down taking out the cooperative culture with it.

Suppose that we measure the payoffs with shares of the pie, meaning the public resources are allocated between the parties. The party who wins the election and aggressively acquires all the resources and gets 1 (100%), and the other party gets 0. In a more cooperative world, assume that each party gets half of the resources when they are in power, and leave the rest to their rival. What should be the payoff associated with getting 50% of resources? If we simply fix it at 0.5, we would have implicitly assumed linear payoffs. That is, any additional share would increase the payoff at the same rate. However, most economic agents' preferences, even the ones of the long-lived agents, such as political parties, demonstrate diminishing returns.

When you've got nothing, even a little bit of resources can make a big difference. It's like going from zero slices of cake to your very first slice. But when you already have most of the cake, getting one more slice isn't quite as exciting. You're already full, and that extra slice doesn't bring you the same joy as the first one did. This is where our square root function comes into play, showing how grabbing an extra 10% of the resources is thrilling when you have nothing but not as thrilling when you've already got most of it.

To capture diminishing returns, let's assume that the payoff to a party can be represented with a square root function. With this payoff function, the payoff of getting only 10% of the resources corresponds to 0.32, while the payoff difference between getting 80% and 90% of the resources is a mere 0.05. This way, an equal division of resources corresponds to approximately 0.7 as a payoff.

Having a payoff with diminishing returns also implies an aversion to taking risks. Imagine the Left Party thinking, "Hey, I could take a chance and get all the public resources, but there's also a solid chance I'll walk away with nothing." On the flip side, the cooperative outcome yields a guaranteed 50% of the resources, which yields 0.7 as the payoff. But if they gamble with a 50/50 chance of walking away with everything or nothing, their expected payoff is just 0.5. Sure, they might win it all, but the risk of getting nothing makes that deal feel much less attractive.

Since we have a dynamic interaction as we had in the OPEC example before, we need to specify the discount factor. Let's fix it at the level of 0.9 as we did before. This way, a party prefers to have at least 90% of the resources now instead of waiting for one more electoral cycle and getting all of them.

Now that we've established that both parties are risk-averse (they don't like gambling away all their resources) and a bit impatient (they'd rather grab what they can now), we can see how this might play out in the long run.

Now, let's think about the present value of future payoffs. If you win this term and every election after that, you could get a 1 this term, plus 0.9 of 1 next term, plus 0.9 squared, and so on. This equals 10 in total. But if you're too greedy and grab everything now, the other party might do the same when they get into power. Therefore, it is never possible in a competitive electoral regime to reach the long-term payoff of 10. Suppose that the incumbent party, whether it is Left or Right, has a 60% probability of winning the next election. This also means that the opposition can win the election with a 40% probability.

Let's start with the uncooperative political culture. Imagine you're the leader of a political party with no trust for the other side. Every time you come to power; you fill every government office with your loyal people. Now, if you're in power, life is good! You take home all the resources this term, so your payoff is 1. But then you start thinking about next term. You've got a 60% chance of staying in power and continuing your winning streak. The value of that future victory is still great, but it's a little less because it's next term, so it's like a payoff of 0.9 times your future payoff, P.

There's also a 40% chance you'll lose and be stuck in opposition, where you do not get anything during that electoral cycle. This future opposition payoff,

O, is still worth something in the longer term, as there is always some chance to win the power back. As there are two outcomes, and they are connected to each other with probabilities, we can calculate the payoffs *P* and *O* by setting up the following couple of linear equations:

$$P = 1 + 0.6 * (0.9 * P) + 0.4 * (0.9 * O),$$
$$O = 0 + 0.6 * (0.9 * O) + 0.4 * (0.9 * P).$$

Solving these two equations simultaneously gives a value of *P* of approximately 5.6 and *O* of approximately 4.4.

Now, imagine two political parties in a country where political harmony is the rule of the day. Instead of the usual "let's grab everything we can while we're in power" routine, the ruling party takes a different approach. They say, "Hey, let's share the pie fairly." They take half of the resources and, in a rare act of goodwill, leave the other half for the opposition – like that friend who saves the last slice of pizza for you, even though you both know they secretly want it.

In this harmonious world, both parties enjoy a smooth, steady payoff of about 0.7 each term. It's way better than the dramatic ups and downs of hoarding everything in one election, only to be left with nothing but crumbs the next. When you add it all up, their cooperative approach results in each party getting a total of 7 units of value over time. That's a 25% improvement compared to the chaotic world of "winner-takes-all," where the ruling party only manages to grab 5.6. Turns out, playing nice and sharing the pie is like opting for a balanced diet over binging at the buffet – it's better for everyone in the long run!

The reason cooperation works so well here is that both parties can sleep a little easier at night, knowing that no matter what happens in the next election, they won't lose it all. It's like agreeing to always share the last piece of cake – no one goes hungry, and everyone's a bit happier. When you remove the "winner-takes-all" chaos, both sides avoid the risk of going home empty-handed, and instead, they enjoy a steady stream of rewards over time.

It's always easier for the opposition to say, "Let's play nice and share," since they're not the ones holding all the goodies. But once the ruling party has their hands on the cookie jar, it's a lot more tempting to grab all the cookies and pretend they forgot about the agreement.

Of course, if the ruling party does sneak away with all the cookies, the opposition will have to switch gears. They'll stop being the friendly, reasonable negotiators and start plotting payback.

Let's imagine our two political parties, the Left Party and the Right Party, are sitting around a table, happily sharing a pie – half for you, half for me. But then, temptation creeps in. The ruling party, eyeing that extra slice, deviates to grabbing all of the sources. Such a deviation breaks down the trust incentivizing the opposition party to switch to uncooperative behaviour. As the strategies switch to the uncooperative ones that we discussed above, we know the long-run consequence of such behaviour; a lower level of 5.6 compared to 7. Therefore, with the current parameters, we can be sure that such a cooperative culture can sustain itself.

Now, let's imagine our political pie-sharing duo – Left Party and Right Party – sitting at the table again. But this time, things are not symmetric. The winning probability for the Right Party, when they are in power is 80%, while the same probability is only 60% when they are in opposition.

In this situation, the Right Party might be tempted to take an extra big slice of the pie, thinking, "Even if the Left Party gets mad and we go back to our old distrustful ways, I'll still be in charge most of the time!" Meanwhile, the

Left Party is looking nervously at that shrinking slice of pie, knowing they don't have the same odds of coming back into power to fix things.

With these new probabilities, the equations for P and O are as follows:

$$P = 1 + 0.8 * (0.9 * P) + 0.2 * (0.9 * O),$$
$$O = 0 + 0.6 * (0.9 * O) + 0.4 * (0.9 * P).$$

Solving these equations gives values of P and O of 7.2 and 5.6, respectively. This final calculation shows that when the Right Party gains power, it might think, "Why bother sharing when I can have the whole pie?" With its stronger grip on power, the temptation to dive headfirst into full patronage and take all the resources becomes too great. Meanwhile, the Left Party, despite its best efforts, simply can't offer a compelling enough reason for the Right Party to keep cooperating. In a country where the Right Party has this kind of edge, the Left Party is left in a frustrating position.

So, it turns out that in this game, full cooperation becomes an unrealistic goal when one side feels too secure in its dominance. The Left Party's best persuasive speeches and promises just won't cut it when the Right Party sees an opportunity to take it all.

******

In the final two chapters of this book, we dive into games of asymmetric information. In signalling games, the player who makes the first move has more information (and a bit of an upper hand), while in screening games it is the second player who holds the key info. The less informed player will use all the available information to make better decisions.

Chapter 15

Signalling Games: Can Edward Smythe Avoid Mad Jack in Disguise?

Edward Smythe was born and raised in the cosmopolitan heart of 19th-century London, a city of contrasts where the grand and the grim coexisted side by side. He was the heir to a modest fortune left to him by his late parents, which allowed him to lead a life of refined tastes and luxuries, particularly in fashion. Edward was known for his impeccable style – every time he stepped out, he donned a crisp black tailcoat over a white waistcoat, paired with polished black shoes, a neatly tied cravat, and a top hat that completed his dapper appearance. His accent, manners, and attire instantly marked him as a true London gentleman, one of the city's polished elites.

Edward had a fondness for visiting his uncle, who lived just two neighbour-hoods away. These visits were a delight for both; Edward would share his latest intellectual pursuits, and his uncle would listen with rapt attention. Their conversations, rich with ideas and laughter, were something Edward cherished deeply. However, for some time now, Edward had not been able to visit his uncle.

A notorious figure by the name of "Mad Jack" had taken up residence in a nearby alley, which was on the very route Edward needed to take to reach his uncle's home. Jack was a fearsome thug, known throughout the area for his wild temper and drunken rages. When he was in his cups, his bellows could be heard from streets away. He made a living by extorting protection money from local shopkeepers, ensuring that everyone paid on time by constantly picking fights and intimidating anyone who dared to cross his path. Mad Jack had a particular disdain for the likes of Edward – gentlemen who, in Jack's eyes, were easy prey. He took great pleasure in roughing up such dandies, especially when there was a crowd to impress.

In those days, London had its own version of the firefighter, known as "The Watchmen." These were brawny men who responded to fires by hauling water pumps through the narrow streets. One such watchman was Tom "Bones" Riddley, a lean, tall fellow whose wiry frame earned him the nickname "Bones." Despite his slender build, no one could beat Tom in a fight.

One evening, a fire broke out in a neighbouring district. Tom, intent on reaching the scene as quickly as possible, found himself taking a shortcut through Mad Jack's alley. Predictably, Jack stepped in his way and snarled, "Oi, where d'you think you're going without my say-so?" Tom, annoyed by the delay, growled back, "And who the devil is you to ask, you drunkard?" Jack, relishing the confrontation, roared, "They call me Mad Jack." He followed this declaration with his favourite taunt: "I'm the man who cuts down anyone who is in my way. Who's gonna test me?"

With the fire blazing ever higher, Tom had no time for games. "Out of my way, you fool, I've got work to do!" he barked. But Jack wasn't one to back down easily and lunged at Tom. The ensuing brawl was fierce but brief – Tom, as many had before, taught Jack a painful lesson. By the next day, word of Mad Jack's defeat had spread far and wide. The once-feared bully had been humbled, and from then on, Jack chose his battles more wisely. He still harassed the gentry, but he stayed away from the watchmen.

Edward, who learned of this incident through his tailor, felt a mix of relief and frustration. It was true that the neighbourhood was buzzing with tales of Mad Jack's fall from grace, but Edward's own reluctance to face Jack had kept him from seeing his uncle for far too long. It was then that an idea struck him: what if he disguised himself as a watchman? Perhaps then he could visit his uncle without fear of being accosted.

Excited by the prospect, Edward hurried to a second-hand shop and purchased a "watchman's coat," a worn cap, and a sturdy pair of boots. He even acquired a rough-looking sash and tucked a makeshift cudgel into it for added effect.

When the day came, Edward eagerly swapped his usual elegant attire for his new outfit. Gone were the polished shoes and fine cravat; in their place, he now wore scuffed boots, a tattered coat, and a grim expression. With his disguise complete, Edward set out for his uncle's neighbourhood, walking with a swagger that belied his true nature.

As he approached Mad Jack's alley, Edward noted Jack lounging outside the local pub, his eyes scanning passersby. Edward stiffened his gait, added a grim expression to his face, and swung his arms loosely as he walked, just as he had seen the watchmen do. Several men sitting outside the pub greeted him with nods and muttered, "Evening, watchman." Edward grunted a reply, trying to sound throaty and indifferent.

Mad Jack eyed him carefully. The events with Tom Riddley had made Jack cautious, and he now scrutinized every watchman who passed through his territory. For some reason, there were more watchmen wandering around the streets after the incident with Tom. Sensing Jack's gaze upon him, Edward casually rested his hand on the cudgel at his waist and continued walking. Jack hesitated, then decided against provoking this "watchman" and turned his attention back to his drink.

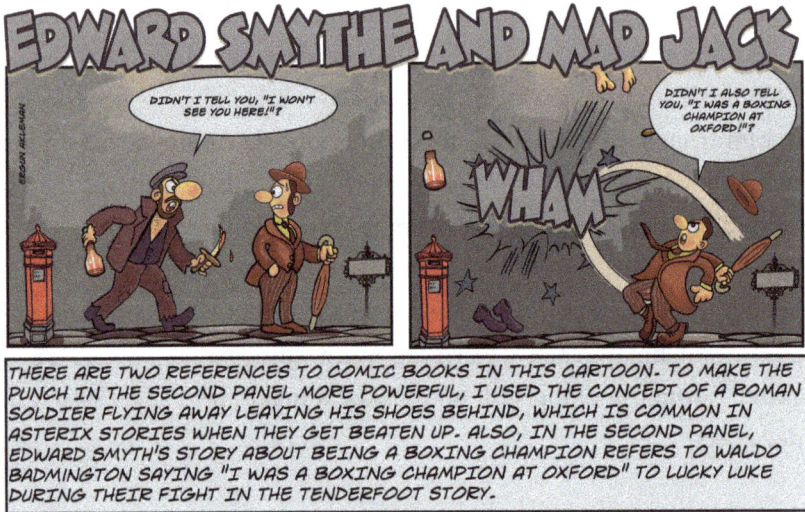

Once Edward was sure he was out of sight, he let out a long breath, his hands trembling as he released his grip on the cudgel. He wiped the sweat from his brow and continued on to his uncle's house.

His uncle was overjoyed to see him. "Edward, my boy, it's been ages! But – what on earth are you wearing?" he asked, his voice a mix of amusement and concern. Edward, still catching his breath, replied, "I'll explain everything, Uncle. It's quite the story."

After settling in and enjoying a cup of tea, Edward recounted his encounter with Mad Jack and his decision to don a watchman's disguise. His uncle listened intently, occasionally nodding in approval. "You've always been clever, Edward," he said with a proud smile. "But tell me, what made you think this plan would work?"

Edward grinned. "It's all a matter of weighing risks and rewards, Uncle both for me and for Jack. If I dressed like a gentleman and walked through that alley, Jack would see me as an easy target and attack. But if

I dressed like a watchman, there was a chance he'd think twice, especially after what happened with Tom. Now, there could be others who are also dressed like a watchman. But if you are not one, it is a bit costly to find the right clothes and convincingly look like a watchman. Therefore, Jack understands that he might be missing some easy targets but staying away from watchmen lookalikes, but still the likelihood of getting smacked by an actual watchman is just too high. It was a gamble for him to stay away from me, and it was a gamble from my side to rely on his risk-aversion; but it paid off."

His uncle chuckled. "Indeed, it did. But what if he had recognized you?"

Edward's smile faltered slightly. "Then it would've been a disaster, Uncle. But I figured the odds were in my favour. Besides, I was ready to run if I had to."

The two of them shared a laugh, and Edward stayed for hours, enjoying the company he had missed so dearly.

A week later, as promised, Edward's uncle decided to return the visit. He too dressed in a watchman's attire, thinking it a clever ruse. But when he arrived at Edward's house, he was met with a shocking sight. Edward was bedridden, his face bruised and swollen.

"Good heavens, Edward! What happened to you?" his uncle cried, rushing to his side.

Edward winced as he tried to sit up. "Ah, Uncle, it's a long story. On my way back home last week, just as I was passing that cursed alley, one of my old servants recognized me. The poor woman was so grateful for the kindness I had shown her in the past that she ran up and embraced me, crying, 'Mr. Smythe! It's so good to see you!' Unfortunately, she said it loud enough for everyone to hear, including Mad Jack. And, well … you can imagine the rest."

His uncle sighed heavily and placed a hand on Edward's shoulder. "Rest, my boy. And don't worry – on my way back, I'll make sure to keep my face well hidden."

******

The game played above is a "signalling game," and it's just like Edward Smythe playing dress-up with high stakes. In signalling games, the player sending the signal – like Edward in his watchman disguise – has to make sure that the message they're sending is loud, clear, and convincing enough to sway the receiver – in this case, the ever-suspicious Mad Jack. For a signal to really work, it needs to be costly enough that it isn't easy for just anyone to pull off. After all, if Edward could simply wear a fake moustache and fool Jack, the whole city would be crawling with moustached gentlemen trying to avoid trouble.

The idea is that Edward, by donning his new "watchman look," is trying to manage Mad Jack's expectations about who he is. The goal is to make Jack think twice before starting anything. If Jack truly believes that Edward is a rough-and-tumble watchman who can handle himself, he'll back off. But if the signal – Edward's outfit – isn't convincing or costly enough (maybe Edward's walk looks a little too refined), Jack might realize something's up and take a closer look.

One of the best-known examples of signalling games happens in business. Imagine a monopolist trying to convince new competitors to stay out of the market. The monopolist keeps prices low to signal that their production costs are low. Competitors, seeing these low prices, may decide it's not worth trying to compete. It's a bit like Edward's "watchman" act, but instead of getting beat up by Jack, the competitor just loses a lot of money.

Another example is in education. Students go through the gruelling process of getting degrees, partly to show potential employers that they can handle complex work. The signal here is the diploma, which says, "Hey, I'm capable of tackling tough challenges!" If getting a degree were easy and required no effort, it wouldn't be a good signal at all.

In Edward's case, he's relying on the perfect Bayesian Nash equilibrium – where the strategies of both players are consistent with their beliefs. Mad Jack must decide: Is this guy really a watchman, or just another gentleman in a tough-looking coat? Edward's strategy is to be so convincing that Jack never bothers to ask. After all, even thugs like Jack have some sense of self-preservation!

Perfect Bayesian Equilibrium: An equilibrium (a concept named after Thomas Bayes) where, given a list of strategies defined over an extensive-form game and the corresponding beliefs of the players, each player's belief at every decision point is formed by Bayesian updating, and all strategies represent the best possible response at every decision point.

In the following chapter, we encounter another fascinating application of the Perfect Bayesian Nash Equilibrium (PBNE). Imagine a seller trying to figure out who among two potential buyers is a big spender and who's on a tighter budget. But instead of just asking, the seller gets creative, using two time-distributed pricing strategies to cleverly weed out the penny-pinchers. It's like a game of "buyer detective," where the seller doesn't have a clue upfront, but by offering different deals over time, they can figure out who's who.

In this new setup, things are flipped from the previous game. Instead of the first player holding all the cards, this time it's the buyer – the person making the second move – who has the juicy inside info. It's a bit like going to a car dealership, knowing exactly how much money you're willing to spend, while the salesperson is trying to guess how deep your pockets are based on whether you go for the immediate flashy deal or wait for the "end-of-the-month blowout sale."

Picture the seller in a Sherlock Holmes hat trying to deduce "Is this buyer ready to splurge on a new convertible, or are they just here for the compact sedan with good mileage?" Meanwhile, the buyers are coolly deciding whether to jump on the first price they see or bide their time for a better offer. It's all about patience and reading the room, or rather, the buyer's wallet!

In the end, the seller's strategy hinges on the perfect Bayesian Nash equilibrium, where the seller has to make their pricing strategy consistent with the clues they pick up from the buyers' reactions. Will they crack the case and figure out who's a big spender and who's playing it safe? Stay tuned as we dive into this price-mystery game!

Chapter 16

Screening Games: Revealing Demand Through Different Prices Over Time

In some of the asymmetric information games, the player with more information does not want to share that information with other players. That could be because her rivals might use that information in a way that could harm her. One of the most common examples of such scenarios is the pricing game between a buyer and a seller, where the buyer knows how much he is willing to pay, but the seller does not. If the seller knew the buyer's willingness to pay, she could post a higher price than what she would without that information. To avoid the higher price, the buyer would not want to share that information. Note that this type of interaction is also related to the economics of the consumer-privacy controversy.

Now, what could the seller do in such a case? The seller could use a sequence of price offers to screen out the buyer's type. Such games are called screening games. The player with less information would check the responses of the other players to update the information she has access to. In the following, we discuss such a scenario.

******

Ethan inherited a house from his recently deceased grandfather. The inheritance came as a relief to Ethan's mother, as it could help cover the costs of Ethan's upcoming wedding and setting up a home. Though Ethan and his girlfriend hadn't been in a rush to marry despite his mother's insistence, the news of the inheritance finally nudged them towards planning a wedding within the next year. This plan meant that the house would need to be sold within that time frame.

Ethan's mother entrusted him with the task of selling the house, but Ethan had no experience in real estate. After browsing some similar properties online, he quickly realized that pricing and negotiating the sale might be beyond his expertise. So, he decided to visit an estate agency in his grandfather's hometown. He took a bus one weekend to meet with Margaret, a seasoned estate agent at the local office. Ethan explained his situation: he and his girlfriend were planning to marry within the year. They could sell the house now, but they were also open to waiting for a better offer; however, the house needed to be sold by the end of the year.

Margaret listened carefully and then explained that the market was rather sluggish. Interest rates had recently risen, and there was a noticeable migration from this small town to larger cities. Unfortunately, the market wasn't expected to improve in the coming year either. "But don't worry," she said, reassuring Ethan that she would find a buyer for the house and would soon prepare a valuation and listing.

A few days later, after confirming there were no outstanding debts or liens on the property and verifying other important details with the local council, Margaret called Ethan to discuss the valuation. According to her calculations, the house could be valued at either £500,000 or £400,000. Ethan was confused at first, as he expected a single price. When he asked why there were two figures, Margaret proudly presented her report.

The report indicated that there were generally two types of buyers interested in houses like this one in the area. The first group consisted of relatively high-income professionals who worked in senior positions at companies located in the nearby city centre. These buyers would be willing to pay £500,000 for such a house. The second group included lower-income workers and civil servants who were more interested in the area's parks, safety, and proximity to local hospitals. This group would be prepared to pay £400,000. The number of potential buyers from each group was roughly equal.

Ethan initially thought they should list the house for £500,000, but Margaret advised against it. Considering the current sluggish market, she felt that listing at this price might attract too few buyers, and if they were from the group willing to pay £400,000, they might struggle to sell the house at all. Ethan, not wanting the house to sit unsold for years, suggested they list it at £400,000 to attract a quick buyer.

Margaret, however, felt this price was too low. They could consider reducing the price to £400,000 if the house was still unsold by the end of the year, but there was no need to lower it just yet. Even if a buyer who was willing to pay £500,000 thought they could get the house for £400,000 by waiting, they might still be willing to pay more than £400,000 to secure it now.

The next day, while preparing the listing, Margaret received a call from a potential buyer, Mrs. Helen Davies, who was interested in the property. Margaret's years of experience allowed her to sense that Helen was serious about buying and likely to negotiate. She asked a few probing questions to determine how much Helen was willing to pay, but Helen, clearly prepared for such inquiries, politely deflected them, noting that the market was slug-gish and she was willing to wait for prices to drop. Margaret responded that the sellers were prepared to wait a year if necessary and were not interested in selling the house at a low price right now.

Helen Davies was a branch manager at a large bank. With her recent promotion, she had been able to save enough and decided it was time to buy a house. While she wasn't in a rush, buying sooner would be preferable, as it would free her from paying rent and dealing with landlords.

After her conversation with Margaret, Helen began to think things over. She was prepared to pay £500,000 for the house, but she was also aware of how sluggish the market was. Margaret had mentioned that the sellers were willing to wait a year. This likely meant that if the house didn't sell, the price might drop to £400,000 by next year.

Helen considered the other potential buyers in the market. Without her recent promotion or if she had been earning less, she wouldn't have been able to afford £500,000. She recalled a recent report from her bank about mortgage applications, which included information on property prices in the area. The report indicated that buyers of houses like this one were prepared to pay between £400,000 and £500,000. Considering the market conditions, it seemed likely that the price would drop to £400,000 if the house remained unsold for another year.

If she could buy the house for £400,000 next year, she would save £100,000, which, given the current 25% interest rate, had a present value of £100,000/(1 + 25%) = £80,000. If she bought the house now for £500,000, she would have nothing left. Therefore, she decided she could offer up to £420,000 for the house right now.

Meanwhile, Margaret was doing similar calculations. Ethan had said they could wait up to a year to sell. This meant they would likely need to lower the price to £400,000 next year. But there was no reason to sell at that price this year. If Helen was only willing to pay £400,000, she could wait and buy it next year for the same amount. But if Helen was willing to pay £500,000, she could save £100,000 by waiting a year, which had a present value of £80,000.

Margaret figured that Helen might be willing to pay an additional £20,000 to secure the house now, leading to a possible sale at £420,000.

Margaret quickly called Ethan to discuss the situation. If they waited a year, they could sell the house for £400,000. However, there was a 50% chance that the buyer was willing to pay £500,000. Ethan suggested they list it for £500,000 now and lower the price to £400,000 next year if it didn't sell. But Margaret disagreed. "If the buyer knows we'll drop the price to £400,000 next year, they'll only be willing to pay up to £420,000 now," she explained. Ethan didn't quite understand where the £420,000 figure came from.

Margaret patiently explained that a buyer willing to pay £500,000 might wait a year to save £100,000, which had a present value of £80,000. This meant that if the price were set at £420,000, the buyer would save £80,000 by purchasing now instead of waiting a year. With this calculation, they could sell the house for £400,000 next year if the buyer could only afford that amount, or for £420,000 now if the buyer was prepared to pay more. The expected average profit would be (£400,000 + £420,000) / 2 = £410,000. "So," Ethan concluded, "if the buyer agrees to £420,000, we'll know they were originally willing to pay £500,000, and we'll have left £80,000 on the table." Margaret nodded in agreement, emphasizing that there was no way around it.

"Since we'll have to lower the price to £400,000 next year, there's no way to convince a buyer with a £500,000 budget to pay more now," she explained.

If they were certain that the buyer was willing to pay £500,000, they could list it at that price and tell the buyer there would be no discount next year. In that case, the buyer might decide to buy the house immediately for £500,000. But what if the buyer could only afford £400,000? They might not sell the house at all, now or next year. Margaret's years of experience had taught her that "The buyer has information that we don't have: their maximum budget. If you want to avoid the risk of not selling the house for a year, you have to leave that £80,000 on the table."

Ethan was surprised at the cost of this information, but in the end, he agreed to list the house at £420,000. However, he had one last question. "Margaret, according to your calculations, £420,000 now is equivalent to £400,000 in a year for the buyer. What if the buyer decides to wait, since it doesn't make a difference?"

Margaret smiled and said that part was easy. The estate agency had a partnership with a furniture and home goods store, offering £500 vouchers to clients who purchased through them. Since clients typically spent much more at the store, the store would give a small commission to the agency. Margaret said, "I'll offer the buyer a £500 voucher if they buy the house now. Even though it's a small incentive compared to the house price, it should be enough to seal the deal."

After the call with Ethan, Margaret phoned Helen Davies and offered the house at £420,000, with the added incentive of a £500 voucher to help furnish the house. Helen was surprised that the number she had written on her notepad exactly matched Margaret's offer. "This agent really knows her stuff!" she thought. She accepted the offer on the spot, pleased to keep the £80,000 difference in her budget and receive the bonus voucher.

Margaret's clever manoeuvring with Helen could easily be likened to a masterful game of chess – only instead of knights and pawns, she used listing prices and furniture vouchers to coax out Helen's true budget. And it worked like a charm. This same pricing strategy, where sellers gradually lower the price to draw out buyers, is a classic technique used to get customers to show their cards.

Now, imagine if instead of selling houses, Margaret was a general trying to figure out just how tough her opponent was. She wouldn't start with a full-blown battle. Instead, she might send out a few scouts or launch a minor skirmish, much like easing into a negotiation. If the opponent crumbles immediately, and she knows she's dealing with a pushover. But if the opponent starts fighting back with surprising strength, Margaret would then think, "Hmm, maybe I'm not dealing with a lightweight here."

And just like in a house sale, the longer the fight goes on, the more Margaret might be willing to offer in terms of concessions to end the conflict peacefully and avoid a full-scale war.

Screening games form the foundation of theories of contract and mechanism design. The details of a contract made with the opposing party can be designed in a way that allows the designer to both gather more information about the other party and increase their own profit. The second-price auction, which we previously discussed (in Chapter 5), can be considered a contract designed for the seller to learn how much the buyers are willing to pay. Another well-known example is insurance policies. Insurance companies do not have complete information about the health or accident risks of customers who are considering purchasing a policy from them. However, by offering different policy options, they can ensure that customers with higher health or accident risks choose different policies from those with lower risks. In this way, the insurance company can understand the risk types of its customers through their choices and make more profit compared to selling the same policy to everyone. While the choice in the illustration above does not directly correspond to a screening game, it gives an idea through a choice similar to selecting an insurance policy: choosing the retirement age.

Chapter 17

Summary and Conclusion

The two practical chapters following the Introduction present innovative game theory applications. The first proposes a referee assignment system for football leagues, like the English Premier League, that incorporates team preferences for greater fairness. The second outlines an AI-based method to reduce chess draws, where moves are scored based on their proximity to optimal play, and the player with the highest score wins in the event of a draw.

In Chapters 4 and 5, where we started to discuss the basic game theory concepts – The Most Iconic Game of All: The Prisoner's Dilemma, Not the First but the Second Price: Auctions – we explored the concept of dominant strategy equilibrium, and then iterated dominance in the next chapter, A Guessing Game: Who Will Win the Beauty Contest? Dominant strategies are intuitive and robust. They are the best strategies for what others choose to do. However, it is often impossible to make predictions by using them, as they don't always exist, i.e., most strategies in most games are not always the best no matter what.

We discussed the most used equilibrium concept, Nash equilibrium, in the following three chapters, Nash Equilibrium: Where Will the Lovers Meet? Fight to the End: From Bertrand Equilibrium to War of Attrition and The Power of Unpredictability: Matching Pennies and Tax Evasion. In the first two of those, there are pure-strategy equilibria, where all players choose the best reply against what others are doing. In the last one, however, the Nash equilibrium is in probabilistic (mixed) strategies. Players are indifferent between the two strategies. Nash equilibrium always exists in a finite game, as John Nash himself proved. This makes it very useful, particularly in applications.

For dynamic games, where players choose their actions one after another, we discussed one of the most intuitive concepts, backward induction. This is a key method to calculate subgame perfect Nash equilibria, one of the most commonly used concepts used in dynamic games. With backward induction, players can trim away non-credible threats from their expectations about the future of the game. In Chapters 10–13, we sampled the range of applications of dynamic games and subgame perfect Nash equilibrium. In Chapter 14, we actually discussed, without naming it, Markov perfect equilibrium, a history-independent version of subgame perfect Nash equilibrium.

In the final two chapters, Chapters 15 and 16, we saw two scenarios where one of the players had more information than the other. These are the games of incomplete information, where we applied the concept of perfect Bayesian equilibrium. In these games, whether the first mover or second mover held the information advantage, the strategies should be optimal at every instance of decision-making, and the resulting gameplay should be consistent with the expectations.

Through the stories and examples in this book, we've tried to guide you through the maze of game theory concepts, showing how they pop up in everyday life moments, negotiations, and even political competition.

In addition to our book, our readers may refer to other game theory books as well. There are some other non-technical books. First, we can note *Introducing Game Theory: A Graphic Guide* by Ivan and Tuvana Pastine. *Game Theory: A Very Short Introduction* by Ken Binmore, *Thinking*

Strategically by Avinash Dixit and Barry Nalebuff, and finally *The Art of Strategy* by Avinash Dixit are other important examples. To dive deeper into the technical details, one can refer to *Game Theory for Applied Economists* by Ribert Gibbons, *A Course in Game Theory* by Martin Osborne and Ariel Rubinstein, *Game Theory* by Drew Fudenberg and Jean Tirole, and *Game Theory: Analysis of Conflict* by Roger Myerson. For behavioural applications and extensions, see *Behavioral Game Theory* by Colin Camerer.

17.1. Final Thoughts

So, what can you take away from this book? Well, for starters, game theory sharpens your analytical thinking as it is a tool for analysis of everyday social interactions. Indeed, game theory is useful in acquiring and sharpening many skills that is predicted by The World Economic Forum[1] to be the top skills among employees by 2025. Skills such as analytical and critical thinking, active learning, problem-solving, and creativity.

Beyond the general brain-boosting benefits, it is possible to derive some general conclusions from the games we discussed. First, instead of making rush decisions, you should consider what everyone else might do. In some cases, it is particularly beneficial to check if there are strategies that are the best to apply irrespective of what others are doing.

Another lesson we learned from the Prisoner's Dilemma is that cooperation is hard. As in the repeated games, cooperation might require establishing long-term relationships to build trust. In contrast, when relationships fall apart, both sides risk dragging each other into a mutual pit of doom as in the wars of attrition. A little communication at the right time, as we saw in the Battle of Sexes game, can prevent mutually destructive outcomes.

---

[1] https://www.weforum.org/agenda/2020/10/top-10-work-skills-of-tomorrow-how-long-it-takes-to-learn-them/.

Of course, everyone will have their own takeaways from this book. The goal is to help you figure out which strategic thinking skills are worth developing in which environments. For instance, it is not beneficial to invest in skills that are dominated by others as they won't give you the best possible outcomes.

We hope this book not only contributed to your strategic skills but also provided an enjoyable reading experience.

A Letter from Nash

J.F. Nash, Jr.
932 Alexander Rd.
Princeton Jct.
New Jersey
08550

Nejat Anbarci
Dept. of Economics
608 O'Brian Hall
SUNY at Buffalo
Buffalo, N.Y.
14260

Nov. 21, 1994

Nejat Anbarci
Dept. of Economics
SUNY at Buffalo

Dear Sir,

I am not actually working in game theory at the present time, in terms of research, so I am not in the best position to advise you.

It seems to me that your study of "Bargaining with a Finite Number of Alternatives" actually brings in elements of "psychosocial" theory. It has always been clear that game theory, with ideal utility measures has abstracted from reality of human behavior in ideally simplified picture.

And also utility measures are related to the idea of creating alternatives by using randomization to mix previously available alternatives.

So these are things to keep in mind.

And I see that you invoke "subgame perfect equilibrium". This is the concept of Reinhard Selten so you could include an appropriate bibliographic reference.

Otherwise, and in general, let me just remark that there is still a bit of controversy in the area of game theory and its applications. So if you have an idea that can be "sold" then you "win", and otherwise you "lose", if your idea fails to sell.

But clearly if you don't have any idea that is new then you've nothing to "sell", in the market of ideas.

So best wishes.

Sincerely Yours,
John Forbes Nash, Jr.

140

Index

www.ingramcontent.com/pod-product-compliance
Lightning Source LLC
Chambersburg PA
CBHW061255220326
41599CB00028B/5655